G000256666

AROUND RYE
IN OLD PHOTOGRAPHS

HAYMAKING ON RYE HILL, probably in the 1890s, showing the rural surroundings of the town before Edwardian development on the northern outskirts. The work-force shown here includes a woman dressed in the contemporary working-class costume – a boater, a long skirt and a big apron. The photograph recalls the description given by the Rye historian, Jeake, in 1678: 'This ancient town is compact as a little City, stored with Buildings, – The Town is of beautiful Prospect to look upon any way'.

AROUND RYE
IN OLD PHOTOGRAPHS

COLLECTED BY
ALAN DICKINSON

ALAN SUTTON
1989

Alan Sutton Publishing
Gloucester

First published 1989

Copyright © 1989 Alan Dickinson

All rights reserved. No part of this publication may be reproduced, stored in a retrieval system, or transmitted, in any form or by any means, electronic, mechanical, photocopying, recording or otherwise, without the prior permission of the publishers and copyright holders.

British Library Cataloguing in Publication Data

Around Rye in old photographs.
1. East Sussex, history
I. Dickinson, A.
942.2′5

ISBN 0-86299-521-3

Front Cover Illustration:

THE LANDGATE, RYE, in the 1890s, showing the Brede and Udimore carrier after it had passed through the arch. The village carrier was an important link between town, country and railway station. It carried both parcels and passengers, although at a very slow pace, and with frequent stops for gossip!

Typesetting and origination by
Alan Sutton Publishing
Printed in Great Britain by
WBC Print Limited

CONTENTS

WEST STREET, RYE, in the early 1890s, being one of a fine collection of photographs by the amateur Hastings photographer, George Woods. The buildings on the left were fifteenth- and sixteenth-century houses, which had been converted into cottages. They were demolished in 1895. The lack of any attempt at modernization indicates a low status. In contrast, the building in the background was the residence of the Misses Pix and bears the scars of its conversion from a shop.

INTRODUCTION

The small town of Rye is well known as a tourist centre, combining a fine heritage of historic buildings with a unique hilltop setting. As one of the Cinque Ports Confederation, along with its sister town of Winchelsea, Rye at one time provided ships for the king in return for privileges. In 1377 it suffered a disastrous raid by the French, and much of the rebuilt medieval town survives to the present day. Popular with artists and writers, it is frequently crowded with visitors of many nationalities.

In the last century Rye was a flourishing port, with sea-going sailing-vessels, and river-barges transporting goods inland. The fishing fleet boasted vessels of many sizes, and seasonal netting was carried out on the shore. Shipbuilding was an important local industry, employing a large work-force, and at one time there were also three breweries in the town, besides an iron foundry and an engineering works. As a market town, as well, Rye was the commercial centre for a wide rural hinterland, and overlapped with other market centres in Kent and Sussex. In 1898 the town was served by 25 carriers, travelling as far as Hastings, Tenterden, Woodchurch and New Romney. Cattle and corn markets were held fortnightly, and there were a multitude of shops, inns, trades and professions, many providing services to an area much wider than the town itself.

In addition to possessing its own Borough Corporation and Law Courts, the town served as an administrative centre for a defined rural area beyond its boundaries. The Poor Law Union, comprising twelve parishes, was later utilized as the area governed by Rye Rural District Council and as a County Court and Magistrates Division. It is this administrative area (shown on the map on page 85) that has been chosen as the boundary for the photographs in this book, most of which were taken between 1890 and 1930. The book aims to present Rye in its rural context and to include links between the town and countryside. The area is diverse, including the shrunken Cinque Port town of Winchelsea, three coastal villages, part of the reclaimed Romney Marshes, three river valleys and nine villages on the wooded hills of the High Weald. The population in 1901 was 11,078, including 3,900 in the Borough of Rye.

Within the rural area the photographs reveal a slower, more ordered way of life than in the town. The squire was a dominant economic and social figure in many parishes, a number of estates being built up or expanded in the nineteenth century. Few farms were owner-occupied, and many were held on twelve-month leases at the whim of the landlord. Mixed farming predominated, with hops, wheat and grazing being prominent. The villages were more self-sufficient than today – the contemporary directories list many vanished shops and trades in addition to those supporting agriculture. In the days before the modern Social Security provisions, the workhouse loomed large as the ultimate destination of those who fell on hard times. A local landowner, Thomas Frewen, recorded in his diary that he was sometimes called upon to loan or give money to callers at the door, and often the squire provided amenities such as a village pump or school. Some parishioners belonged to village 'slate' clubs, which provided an annual treat and a measure of security.

Changing times are indicated in the photographs by hints of the economic shift in the present century away from farming and industry towards tourism. As early as 1902 land at Camber was sold with 'sites suitable for bungalows', and between the wars 'plot-land' development proliferated on or near the sand dunes at Camber and the shingle ridges at Winchelsea Beach. In many cases old buses or railway carriages were converted, while other plots were never developed further and have reverted to scrub. More affluent visitors included golfers and well known authors and artists, thus boosting the boarding-house and hotel trades. A growing band of part- and full-time residents populated new suburbs on Rye Hill and restored cottages in the town, while shops increasingly catered for the tourists. The town became more conscious of its past: a Committee for the Preservation of the Ancient Buildings of Rye was formed in 1895, and a museum, first projected in 1889, was founded in 1928. Rural estates, meanwhile, hit by falling rents and taxation, were increasingly broken up and sold after 1918, largely to tenant farmers and sometimes as select building plots. Improved road communications, including motor-bus services from the 1920s, were coupled with a decline in village shops and services.

This book has provided an opportunity to publish for the first time several early photographs of Rye, as well as examples of the work of two skilled amateurs. George Woods (1852–1934) produced outstanding material on rural, maritime and Rye subjects, often showing people at their everyday work. John Henry Chatterton (1834–1928) was a native of Rye who returned regularly from London in his old age for holidays, recording local scenes and events, often with the subjects being unaware of the camera. Among the professional photographers in Rye, Edwin Whiteman, working between c.1890 and c.1915 was the most prolific, recording local landscapes, snow scenes and official events for postcards, in addition to his portrait work.

DEDICATION

To my wife Jean and son James, who arrived during the final stages of the preparation of this book.

Rye – Ancient Town

The following photographs illustrate the streets and buildings of an ancient Cinque Port town adapted to the needs of a bustling market centre of the nineteenth and twentieth centuries. Most of the medieval defensive monuments and public buildings survive within a modified grid of cobbled streets. The town was, however, largely rebuilt during its time of greatest prosperity in the early sixteenth century. Many of these buildings, largely refaced during the Georgian period, have survived, despite wartime bombing. The nineteenth century saw many houses sub-divided with additional cottages added on behind them. Ownership was fragmented at this time, although there was a tendency for investment by leading businessmen.

THE LANDGATE, C.1870. The fourteenth-century gate survived the sale and demolition of monuments carried out by the eighteenth-century Corporation. In the sixteenth century, the street had developed as a suburb, outside the defensive ditch and walls of the town. The presence of the Tower Inn is recorded from 1846 to 1901; Thomas Jordan had succeeded William Henry Mills as landlord by 1874. The picture post-dates 1863, when the clock was added to the Landgate.

THE LANDGATE FROM HILDERS CLIFF, c.1880. This road, near the cliff edge, was improved in the 1860s by the Corporation – it is their railings which can be seen on the right. Tower Forge, adjoining the gate, was partly rebuilt in 1878 – the figure in the long apron standing in the street was probably the blacksmith, Silas Winton. The rotund character in a long smock was probably a farm carter or shepherd.

THE MONASTERY FROM CONDUIT HILL, 15 June 1901. The building was the chapel of the Augustinian friary, which was put to many secular uses following the Dissolution. In 1901 it was a Salvation Army barracks and an artist's studio. One of Rye's cobbled streets, Conduit Hill had been the main route of the town's piped water supply from at least the sixteenth century, and the eighteenth-century pump-house may be seen at the foot of the hill.

A VISITOR TO RYE, C.1907. Miss Clements of London, recorded by the amateur photographer J.H. Chatterton. The double-fronted building in the centre was the Oak Inn, which had a short life in the 1900s before becoming tea rooms. Flanking it in 1859 were Broad's candle factory on the left, and the factory's warehouse on the right. By 1899 the factory was also functioning as a grocer's shop, run by the former manager, George Pellett.

AN INFORMAL SCENE IN THE HIGH STREET, 1 June 1907. The commerical centre of the town has always been busy with pedestrians. Freeman, Hardy & Willis was one of the earliest multiple retailers to be established in the town, being first listed in 1887. The firm moved from No. 22 to No. 23 High Street, shortly before the date of this photograph.

THE HIGH STREET LOOKING EAST, late nineteenth century. The delivery cart belonged to a baker, Charles House, who was listed in the directories printed between 1885 and 1899 as trading at No. 89 – the building remains a baker's shop today. The photographer's reference '8581' suggests a possible date in 1885.

THE HIGH STREET WITH MOTOR TRAFFIC, 1937. The shop-fronts have changed over the years, but the buildings remain largely as they would have been in the eighteenth and nineteenth centuries. The three well-known multiple retailers, Mence Smith (ironmongers), Flinns, and Boots, were all established in Rye in the 1930s.

THE HIGH STREET, DECORATED FOR THE CORONATION OF GEORGE V, 1911. The building on the left was Bank House, home of an eighteenth-century solicitor and town clerk, Jeremiah Curteis. The house was demolished to make way for a branch of Woolworths in the 1930s.

MRS SHARPE AND THE TOWN CLERK, a chance meeting in Lion Street, c.1907. Mrs Sharpe was probably the wife of George Thomas Sharpe of Church House, Church Square, listed as a private residence from 1887 to 1911. Walter Dawes (1845–1930), town clerk from 1882 to 1924, was a partner in the Rye firm of solicitors, Dawes, Son & Prentice.

ST MARY'S PARISH CHURCH FROM LION STREET in the 1900s. The church tower with its squat spire forms the summit of the hilltop town. The eighteenth-century Quarter Boys strike the quarter hours only – not the hours. All the shops on the left side of the street were occupied by Delves & Son: in descending order, a draper's, a china shop, a shoe shop, a furniture warehouse and a men's outfitter's.

THE TOWN HALL, MARKET STREET in the 1900s. Built in 1742, to the design of Andrews Jelf (architect of the first Westminster Bridge), this building was funded by a loan from the town's two Members of Parliament, a loan never repaid. In the 1900s, the first-floor rooms were used for council meetings and sessions of court. The ground floor, originally a market, housed the borough fire station and a magistrates' office.

A LADY DRIVES OUT – the corner of Church Square and Pump Street in the 1900s. The vehicle is a phaeton, with space for shopping and an umbrella. The lady bears a resemblance to the Mrs Sharpe in the photograph on page 13. This was the pitch of 'Blind Bob', a beggar found on many old photographs of the period.

THE YPRES TOWER AND ADJOINING COTTAGES, c.1900. A common postcard subject but unusual in its relatively early date and wide angle of view. The tower was built in the thirteenth century and functioned as the town's jail from 1494 to 1891. The left-hand pair of cottages was rebuilt soon after the date of this photograph.

THE SOUTH SIDE OF CHURCH SQUARE, c.1900. This was traditionally a poor part of the town. In common with other streets, nineteenth-century development had been carried out behind the medieval houses. The urchins may have lived in one such development, Hucksteps Row, a slum area which was partly cleared during the 1920s, when the façades were rebuilt in a timber-framed style. The lantern on the left belonged to the police station, built in 1891 and in use until 1966. The Jolly Sailor was a boarding house for itinerants.

THE JUNCTION OF CHURCH SQUARE AND WATCHBELL STREET, c.1860. Well known as one of Rye's cobbled streets, Watchbell Street ran along the edge of the hill, allowing far-reaching views for defensive purposes. The shop on the right was occupied by Mrs Sarah Ruby from the 1850s, evidently as a grocer's – the goods visible in the window included 'Fry's Cocoa'.

WATCHBELL STREET, LOOKING EAST, in the 1890s. The channel in the centre of the street indicates the lack of piped surface-water drainage in a mainly residential street. In the far distance is Rye's Methodist chapel, bombed during the last war. The posters advertise respectively: Col. A.M. Brookfield, successful Conservative candidate in the 1892 and 1895 parliamentary elections, and H. Horrell, a chemist.

TWO WELL-DRESSED LADIES OUT WALKING at the end of Watchbell Street in the 1900s. Although the buildings have disappeared, the scene is instantly recognizable. Gas lighting was provided in the town from at least the 1850s. The Jubilee Almshouses were converted from cottages by public subscription in 1897.

WEST STREET in the 1890s. A well known landmark, the crooked chimney was added in the sixteenth century to Grene Hall, later used as the town's Customs House. The garden wall on the right was that of Lamb House, home of the Lamb family, who dominated Rye's political life in the eighteenth century. Note the wooden gutters.

MERMAID STREET in the 1890s. The fine house on the right of this steeply sloping street was built in 1576 and was later the home of Samuel Jeake II, a seventeenth-century scholar and diarist. The building further down, on the left, with steps and railings, was the mid-eighteenth century Baptist chapel. Jeake's storehouse adjoined on the left and still bears an astrological chart for the date of its foundation in 1689.

THE STRAND IN THE DAYS OF HORSE-DRAWN TRANSPORT, c.1920. The timber building was the Old Ships Stores, built in the eighteenth century and occupied, until its collapse in the 1920s, by Henry John Gasson & Sons, government contractors. The other warehouse belonged to Edgar L. Stonham, corn merchant. The cats lying on the weighbridge were no doubt useful in controlling rats.

WINCHELSEA ROAD AND THE TILLINGHAM BRIDGE, C.1920. The lock was the tidal limit of the River Tillingham and was rebuilt, with a wider bridge, in the early 1920s. The building was the showroom, boardroom and offices of the Rye Gas and Coke Company Ltd, founded in 1839. The manager's house lay on the right, and the gasworks to the rear.

THE BREDE BRIDGE AND SLUICE in the 1890s. Situated on the road to Rye Harbour, this was the tidal limit of the River Brede, navigable for barges as far as Brede Wharf. The mast in the centre of the photograph is that of a trading vessel which has been manoeuvred into the approach to the sluice by ropes and warping posts in order to allow her to turn round and sail out of the harbour.

FERRY ROAD on a wet day in the 1910s. This was the route to Battle via the Udimore ridge. The road had been the centre of a small suburb since the sixteenth century – a house of this date has been recently discovered here. The four businesses shown include George Henry Saddleton, a butcher who traded briefly in the 1910s, Harry Norman Chester, a boot repairer, and Blackman & Baker, builders, contractors and undertakers, a firm established in the 1900s.

CINQUE PORTS STREET, c.1915. Rye's secondary commercial street was greatly developed in the nineteenth century. The building on the left belonged to Ellis Bros., builders, monumental masons and builders' merchants. Beyond were the Cinque Ports Hotel and assembly rooms (with the pair of chimneys). On the far right of the picture Thomas Gasson's furniture stores can be seen.

FISHMARKET ROAD, before 1903, showing public provision of open space and landscaping. The Town Salts were embanked in 1834 and appropriated as a recreation ground. On the opposite side of the road, the picture shows the parade and steps built in 1864–5 by the Corporation at Hilders Cliff, overlooking the Salts. The pollarded willows provided cuttings for further planting on the Salts in 1855.

RYE CEMETERY, c.1880. Opened in 1855 to serve both Rye and Rye Foreign, following closure of the churchyard at Rye, the cemetery was divided into two sections, each with a chapel: that for Nonconformists on the left, and that for Anglicans on the right. The ornate wooden kerbs have since disappeared. The fencing, against which a man is seen leaning, was removed before 1897.

The Port of Rye

Rye already possessed a major harbour, 'The Camber', in the sixteenth century. Silting and reclamation reduced its capacity and there has been a history of conflict between maritime and landed interests. By 1898 the harbour was governed by a commission, composed of town councillors, householders, ship-owners and land-drainage representatives. The commission had to struggle to keep the channels clear despite revenue from a busy coasting-trade in coal, corn, timber, shingle and hops. The Rye shipyards were renowned for the quality of the sailing-trawlers that they supplied to North Sea ports.

THREE VESSELS ON THE ROTHER AT RYE HARBOUR, c.1900. In the foreground, the *John Bull*, with sails furled, is moored against piles. A fast coasting-schooner, she was nearly too large for the harbour. Behind, the *Three Brothers* (RX153) can be seen sailing up river. This was built at Rye in 1896 as a sailing-trawler; she was later converted to a cruising-yacht. The paddle-steam trawler on the right, *Crusader* (16RX), was built in 1875 and bought in 1884 by a consortium of Rye merchants before being broken up in 1904.

THE FISHMARKET, Rye, in the 1890s. The pole was probably an old ship's mast used to suspend nets for drying and repair, an activity also recorded at Pole Marsh, Ferry Road. RX70 was one of the larger Rye sailing-trawlers, with a beam trawl hung over her starboard side. The small boat was possibly a pleasure-craft. The fishermen are seen wearing the jerseys and bowler hats common among boatmen of the time.

SAILING-TRAWLERS AT THE FISHMARKET, Rye, c.1900. The rigging of RX150 is here seen undergoing repair. In addition the photograph includes no fewer than fourteen fishermen grouped on the bank and the landing stage, reflecting a late nineteenth-century harbour commissioner's complaint that, 'The fishing smacks are getting more numerous, more troublesome, less under control'.

SAILING-PUNTS AT RYE HARBOUR in the 1890s. The punts were small, open fishing boats used by the poorer fishermen for all types of fishing, including long-lining. Some carried oars, hung over the sides, and oil-lamps for night-time drift-netting. The boats were lug-rigged, with the sail fore of the mast.

A SAILING-TRAWLER LEAVING THE HARBOUR MOUTH in a strong north-westerly wind. The boat was a ketch, with fore and mizzen-masts, gaff-rigged to provide manoeuvrability in the river. Such vessels continued in service until about 1930, when the industry was hit by the economic slump.

A STEAM-TRAWLER LEAVING THE HARBOUR MOUTH, probably in the 1920s. Steamers first appeared in the Rye fleet in the 1880s and became more numerous after 1900 – to the annoyance of becalmed Hastings fishermen. In common with the sailing-trawlers, steam-vessels disappeared around 1930. The fleet reappeared with smaller, diesel-powered boats after the Second World War.

MENDING A TRAWL-NET AT THE POINT, RYE HARBOUR, C.1900. The village grew up in the early nineteenth century, at what was then the mouth of the Rother, when high tides extended to the buildings on the left. These early buildings included The Ship Inn and, on the left, a Customs House, with watch-tower and mortuary. The William the Conqueror, on the right, was opened around 1860.

KEDDLE-NET FISHING AT CAMBER in the 1900s. The nets were erected on flat, sandy shores between Romney Marsh and Pevensey to take advantage of the mackerel which swam near the coast in the summer. Often operated by farmers, regular fishermen saw the nets as a hazard to boats and a waste of fish stocks. The nets were attached to stakes 11 ft high, set out in a straight line between high- and low-water marks. Fish encountered the obstruction and swam seawards, to be caught in a circular pound. The industry died out around 1930 due to dwindling shoals and falling demand. Above: netting fish within the pound. Below: loading the catch into a high-wheeled cart.

FRESHWATER FISHING. Netting grey mullet on the River Rother above Iden Lock in the 1920s.

'BLUE BOULDER PICKING' AT RYE HARBOUR, c.1919. This was a low-paid, piecework industry, which supplemented variable incomes from fishing. Blue flints, used in the pottery industry, were gathered on the shingle at Rye Harbour and Winchelsea Beach and brought to the railway at Rye Harbour in small, gaff-rigged boats. The picture shows one such boat being unloaded by a member of the Cutting family.

G. & T. SMITH'S ROCK CHANNEL SHIPYARD, RYE, in the 1900s. A major industry in the town, shipbuilding reached a peak in the late nineteenth century, employing several hundred men and building mainly sailing-trawlers for the North Sea ports. It was said that 'Rye-built was a hallmark second to none', local oak contributing to the high quality of the ships. Hit by competition from iron trawlers, shipbuilding had almost disappeared in Rye by 1918.

SHIPBUILDERS AT G. & T. SMITH'S YARD at the end of the nineteenth century. The men, proudly carrying the tools of their trade, were working on the frames for a Lowestoft trawler.

THE LAUNCH OF THE *SARAH COLEBROOKE*, 1913. The event was reported by the *Hastings & St Leonards Observer* on 9 October 1913: 'Great interest was manifested at Rye last week in the launch of the auxiliary motor coasting vessel, *Sarah Colebrooke*. The craft is one of the largest, as well as the first motor propelled vessel ever laid down at Rye, and her construction is evidence of the progress of the shipbuilding industry of the Ancient Town. She has been built for the Mayor (Cllr W.E. Colebrooke, JP) by the well-known firm of Messrs. George & Thomas Smith Limited, Rock Channel Shipyard, and the christening ceremony was undertaken by His Worship's mother, Mrs Colebrooke, whose name the vessel has been given.'

William Colebrooke (1856–1926) was a leading Rye coal merchant and shipowner. In the First World War the *Sarah Colebrooke* was used as a 'Q-ship' or anti-submarine decoy, being reinforced with sandbags and steel plates and armed with three-inch guns, machine-guns and explosives. In one engagement her gun-house was shelled, but she returned fire within seconds with apparently lethal results.

HIGH WATER AT RYE HARBOUR, c.1900. A busy maritime scene showing a Rye trawler, *The Pert* (RX181), sailing past commercial moorings towards the fishing boats moored in the background. Of the two trading vessels on the left, one was a brigantine, with a square-rigged foremast and fore-and-aft-rigged mainmast. The ship on the right was a Baltic trader, a barkentine, having three masts, one square-rigged. The cargo vessels were probably waiting to unload on to smaller barges, or to moor at Rye, the unique silhouette of which is visible in the background.

HIGH TIDE AT THE STRAND QUAY, RYE, in the 1890s. A charming study by George Woods, showing a fishing smack sailing up to the quay with her beam trawl hanging over the port side, past a large rowing boat and some smaller craft. A number of people were enjoying the scene from the shore, including several children clambering among the nets, which had been spread out on the bank to dry. On the far left of the photograph can be seen one of Vidler & Sons' coal warehouses, built in 1804 by Lamb & Batchelor, timber and coal merchants. Next to it was the Grist Mill, built between 1771 and 1840 and occupied by Edgar L. Stonham, a corn merchant, from the late 1880s. In the centre was Strand House, then the home of Alderman John Holmes, a retired shipbuilder who served 53 years on the town council. The house was destroyed, along with adjoining buildings, in an air raid in 1942. The area to the right had formerly been Hessel & Holmes' Shipyard. This photograph is also a reminder of the fact that boats may only enter and leave the harbour for a short period either side of the high tide.

BARGES AT THE STRAND QUAY in the late 1920s. Two ketch-rigged coasting-barges are shown moored at the quay, with a Rother barge between them. The *Mazeppa* hailed from Ipswich and traded in coal. Behind, two motor lorries appear to be unloading timber at T. Hinds & Sons' timber and slate yard. Timber was stacked in the open on both sides of the road still known as 'The Deals'. The tall buildings in the background were Stonham's corn warehouses, adjoining the harbour-master's office on the quayside. To the right Vidler & Son's coal warehouses and the Grist Mill may be seen. The coal office on the left was built as Rye's Customs House in 1855, remaining in use until the mid-1920s when the office moved to Cinque Ports Street.

VIDLER & SONS' WAREHOUSE AT THE STRAND, c.1860. Founded in 1820 by John Vidler, this firm was at one time Rye's leading general merchant and shipowner, occupying most of the warehouses at The Strand. The notice in the window reads 'Lloyds Agent, Admiralty Receiver and -?- Consulate'. The warehouse was probably built in 1736.

VIDLER & SONS' OFFICES AT THE STRAND. The stove-pipe hat suggests that this photograph was taken soon after the offices were built in 1862. The firm sold off the corn side of its business in the late 1880s but carried on trading as coal merchants until the 1930s. The warehouse on the left was later used by H.J. Gasson & Sons for the manufacture of nets and tarpaulins.

UNLOADING WAGONS AT STONHAM'S WAREHOUSES in the 1930s. Grain was delivered by farmers for cleaning, storage or sale and hoisted by hand to the upper floors. The tall building was added to the Great Warehouse, on the right, around 1800, the remaining buildings dating from soon after. The photograph was taken after the conversion of the harbour-master's office to public lavatories in the early 1930s.

THE CRUSADER TOWING A LADEN BARGE on the Rother near the Fishmarket, Rye, in the 1890s. The paddle-steam trawlers produced additional income by acting as tugs in the confined channel of the harbour. The vessel on the left was probably undergoing repair at the Rother Ironworks Company's Patent Slipway.

QUANTING A RYE RIVER-BARGE on the Rother, probably near Scots Float Sluice, Playden, in the 1920s. The barges were operated at this period by Vidler & Sons between Rye and Bodiam and on the River Brede. The mast was lowered across the hold, the sail being used only when the wind was favourable for sailing in a confined waterway.

THE ROTHER FERRY, near Northiam, in the 1890s. It is believed that the ferry served a brickyard near the south bank of the river, the stacks of wood possibly being fuel for the kilns. The house was New Barn, on the north bank at Newenden in Kent. Note the mother and daughter with baby standing near the outside privy.

THE RYE FERRYMAN in the 1890s. The ferry plied from the Fishmarket to East Guldeford and Camber before the building of the Monkbretton Bridge in 1893. It also provided a short-cut for fishermen on their way to Rye Harbour. The ferryman seen here tarring a rowing boat was probably F. Page senior, whose cottage survives at the southern end of the Fishmarket.

THE RYE HARBOUR FERRYMAN, c.1920. The ferry served the crews of fishing and trading vessels moored on both banks of the Rother, in addition to visitors to Camber. The ferryman is seen standing at the door of his hut wearing leather boots with iron soles.

THE RYE HARBOUR FERRY, c.1923. The ferryman ran two boats, the one illustrated having a keel for use at high tides, the other being flat-bottomed for low tides.

CAMBER COASTGUARD STATION in the 1900s. The Coastguard Service employed a sizeable and mobile workforce, drawn from all over the country. The Camber station was built in 1866 and included a boat-house, watch-house and ammunition store. There were other coastguard stations at Winchelsea Beach, Rye Harbour and Broomhill; the Camber station closed around 1910.

SEA DEFENCE WORKS AT WINCHELSEA BEACH in the 1940s. Until the 1930s the foreshore had been protected by timber groynes and faggots, but several buildings had been lost to the sea. In 1934/5 a timber framework was built and filled with shingle. The photograph shows an example of faggot-thatching, a traditional technique, which was used to repair the defences before the present sea-wall was built in the late 1940s.

SECTION THREE

Crafts and Industries

In a horse-drawn age, the blacksmith, wheel-wright and saddler were univer-sal. There were four smiths in Rye in 1898 and each village usually had at least one. Ironworking on a larger scale was also carried out in the town. Food-processing industries included the breweries in Rye and a multitude of windmills in the area. Builders ranged from established firms in Rye to small, village tradesmen, with brickyards and farm quarries supplying some mater-ials. Also included in this section are photographs of the newer Rye 'industries' of tourism and the arts.

MARTIN'S WHEEL-WRIGHT SHOP, BROAD OAK, BREDE, in 1903. Stephen Martin was listed in 1905 as a wheel-wright, agricultural engineer and assistant overseer, a paid part-time office under the Poor Laws. By 1934 Martin & Ashdown had added building and decorating to the business. The wheel-wright's shop was a popular meeting place for farmers to discuss parish affairs.

E. PERCY S. JONES,

ENGINEER and BOILER MAKER,
Iron and Brass Founder,

RYE, SUSSEX.

Agent for all the leading
AGRICULTURAL IMPLEMENT MAKERS.

STEAM, GAS and OIL ENGINES.
Both New and Second-hand.

Pumps and Pumping Machinery.

IRON FENCING, GATES, TOMB RAILINGS
IN ANY DESIGN.

HOT WATER SUPPLY, or HEATING APPARATUS
for Houses, Conservatories, etc.

Write for quotations.

Patent Slip for Steam Yacht and Launch Repairs.

ADVERTISEMENT FOR THE ROTHER IRONWORKS, RYE, from a trade directory of 1907. The business was founded in 1863 and soon suffered financial loss after starting a marine department, although their two iron ships were considered to be of 'excellent design, adaptability, and seaworthiness', due to the skills of the manager, Samuel Clark, inventor of the twin-screw. The firm was bought in the 1880s by the then manager, Percy Jones, and is still in business.

STAFF AT THE ROTHER IRONWORKS, c.1887. The photograph shows the rear of the foundry buildings at the junction of Fishmarket Road and South Undercliff. The works had departments for founding, forging, fitting, machining, pattern- and boiler-making, with a Patent Slip for ship repairs. In the background are the Gun Garden, Ypres Tower and Inn, and the back of the Methodist chapel.

MUSHETT'S FORGE, WISH STREET, RYE, c.1930. The forge was marked with a distinctive overhanging canopy on a map of 1859. It was run from the 1890s as a part of the business of Richard Milsom, 'General and Manufacturing Ironmonger, Blacksmith, Gas & Water Fitter, Metal Plate Worker, Gunsmith and Ammunition Dealer', based at Nos. 28 and 29 High Street. By 1924 it had been leased to Frank Mushett.

FORGE INTERIOR AT BREDE in the 1920s. One of two blacksmiths in Brede in 1905, William Horton was still in business in 1934, by which time a new generation of metalworkers was represented by H.C. Hartnell Ltd, 'Automobile, Agricultural and General Engineers'.

EAST GULDEFORD BREWERY in the 1900s. Established by the Lamb family in the eighteenth century, Chapman's Brewery was situated on the Rother at Military Road, just within East Guldeford. Other breweries included Bowen's at Landgate and, until the 1840s, Meryon & Holloway's at The Strand. The introduction of the railway led to competition from outside breweries, and Chapman's was demolished in 1911, though part of it remains as a tennis club.

BECKLEY FURNACE MILL IN THE LATE NINETEENTH CENTURY. A water-mill was recorded at this site, just within Brede, from the sixteenth century, functioning as an ironworks from 1650 to 1796. The corn mill was built around 1805 and run by three generations of the Miller family until its destruction by fire in 1909. There appears to have been a steam engine for periods of drought.

PLAYDEN WINDMILL, c.1905. Dating from the early nineteenth century, the mill was a post windmill, the whole building revolving around a post which was set on a framework within the roundel. A mound and former bakehouse relating to two other windmills on Rye Hill survive nearby. The Playden mill was worked, with a bakery, by Edgar Thorpe until 1915, when the assistant, Arthur Luck, left for war service. Sadly it was demolished to make way for a new house in 1952.

PEASMARSH WINDMILL in the 1900s. Situated at Flackley Ash, this mill was of the later 'smock' type, less numerous in this area, where only the cap revolved to face the wind. Operated in 1905 by Charles J. Banister, with a bakery and mill at Northiam, the Peasmarsh mill was demolished before the First World War.

ALTERATIONS AT THE PIPEMAKERS ARMS, RYE, c.1907. Situated at the junction of Wish Street and Wish Ward, this building was recorded as a public house from 1844. It is here seen undergoing a face-lift, with Edwardian gabled barge-boards replacing the earlier hiplets. The cottages on the left were largely destroyed by bombing in the Second World War. Note the timber-and-rope scaffolding resting in barrels.

EMPLOYEES OF ELLIS BROS AT IDEN in 1925, including, on the left, Frank Caister, a carpenter, and on the right, Will Caister. The men were building Burnt Oak Manor at Boonshill Lane for Lewis Linnett, a London accountant – a reminder of the additional business provided after the 1900s by high-class residential properties, many for weekend and holiday occupation only.

QUARRYING FOR STONE AT BREDE, probably in the 1900s. In addition to timber, many farms provided building materials as a sideline, including bricks, tiles and lime. In 1934 Gerald Baker was listed at Reysons Farm as a 'farmer and blue stone quarry owner: crazy paving, rockery and roadmaking stone'. The stone was probably the hard 'Tilgate Stone' found in the Wadhurst clay.

DOROTHY CARTER'S JAM FACTORY AT IDEN in the 1930s. The business was started at Miss Carter's parents' house in Iden before the First World War. It later moved to a cottage at Rye Foreign and occupied half of the Old Mission Room as a jam store. The Still Room at Iden was built in 1929, and remains in business today.

E.F. BENSON DISTRIBUTING JUBILEE MUGS OUTSIDE THE TOWN HALL, 1935. Edward Frederick Benson (1867–1940) was one of many literary figures who lived in Rye; others included Henry James, Radcliffe Hall, and Conrad Aiken. Benson lived at Lamb House and was the author of several books, including the satirical *Miss Mapp* novels, which depicted life in the town. He was mayor from 1934 to 1936. The building in the background was a five-storey gazebo, built in the grounds of Tower House, West Street, in 1768.

HOWARD AND MARY STORMONT AT THEIR STUDIO IN RYE, c.1910. Among artists associated with Rye were the Stormonts, who lived and worked from 1898 at Ypres Studio, Ockmans Lane, painting rural and maritime scenes and exhibiting at the Royal Academy. Mrs Stormont endowed the Rye Art Gallery, opened at her former home in 1965.

FIRST-CLASS
FARM HOUSE,
APARTMENTS,
TENNIS,
CROQUET,
PRIVATE
FISHING,
OWN DAIRY.

Bosney House Iden, Rye, Sussex.

A COUNTRY GUEST HOUSE – BOSNEY HOUSE, IDEN, c.1900. Rye became popular as a weekend and holiday area, especially after the opening of the golf course in 1894. In addition to the appearance of guest houses, public houses increasingly offered accommodation for visitors, cyclists and motorists.

WAITING TO SEE THE FRESCO, 13 July 1910. From the late nineteenth century, visitors were increasingly attracted to Rye by its history and archaeology. The fresco was discovered in 1905 at the sixteenth-century Flushing Inn, Market Street. The photograph shows members of the Hastings and St Leonards Natural History Society on an excursion to Winchelsea and Rye.

THE SEASIDE — children on a beach near Rye, probably in the 1900s. The children appear to be playing with a younger sibling's perambulator. Camber Sands and Winchelsea Beach became popular seaside destinations, and bungalow settlements grew up, especially from the 1920s.

SECTION FOUR

Commercial Life

Photographs abound of shops in Rye and the surrounding area, ranging from small traders starting in their front rooms to long established businesses in the town serving the wealthier townspeople and farmers. The delivery of goods by hand or horse-drawn vans was a common feature. The arrival of multiple retailers is also recorded, while the growth of business empires in the town such as Delves & Son has already been encountered on page fourteen. Inns and hotels existed in almost every street in Rye and the postal system provided a frequent, even same-day, service in the heyday of the postcard. There was an increasing need for professional services, especially estate agents, who managed surrounding estates and catered for new residential demands.

LONGLEY'S CORNER, RYE, c.1880. Isaac Longley took over an established grocery business at the junction of Ferry Road and Cinque Ports Street in the 1860s. He is seen here with his staff and delivery van. A popular member of the Congregational Church, he died in 1899 during his year of office as mayor, the shop later being demolished.

THE INTERNATIONAL STORES, RYE, in the 1920s. The International Tea Company was one of the earliest household names to become established in Rye, taking over a house at No. 87 High Street in about 1890. The firm rebuilt the premises and, after about 1910, also ran Longley's grocery shop at Ferry Road. Above: the manager Ernest Rhodes, staff and delivery man outside the High Street premises. The van can just be seen on the right. Below: interior of the High Street store, showing the long counters required for service of items by assistants.

A LIPTON'S TEA DISPLAY AT BECKLEY STORES, probably in the 1900s. An example of blanket advertising by a household name. The stores were run by William Maynard as a grocer's, linen draper's and post office in 1905. Note the worn steps to the shop door.

HERBERT BAKER'S SHOP AT PEASMARSH, c.1900. Another example of the common combination of grocer and draper at village shops. The shop was one of four groceries in Peasmarsh in 1905.

FRED CRISFORD DELIVERING MILK FOR THE PEASMARSH DAIRY FARM, in the 1900s. The vehicle was a float, entered from the rear, and drawn by a small pony. Mrs Ellen Fuggle was listed as a dairy farmer at the Hermitage, on the Peasmarsh Place Estate, in 1905.

WINCHESTER'S BUTCHER'S SHOP AT NO. 16 LANDGATE. The impressive display was for Christmas 1928 or 1929. An established butcher's shop, the business was acquired in the mid-1920s by James Winchester (centre). By 1934 the assistant, Herbert Cheesman (left) had taken over. On the right, with motor cycle and side-car, was Charles Muggridge, slaughterman and delivery man.

ASHBEE'S BUTCHER'S SHOP AT NO. 100 HIGH STREET, c.1910. Henry Ashbee started trading at Ferry Road in the 1880s before moving to No. 2 East Street and then to prime High Street premises in the 1900s. A butcher's since at least the 1850s, the High Street shop is still in business and retains its splendid shop-front with canopy and hooks. Note the telephone number; telephones were introduced into Rye in 1904.

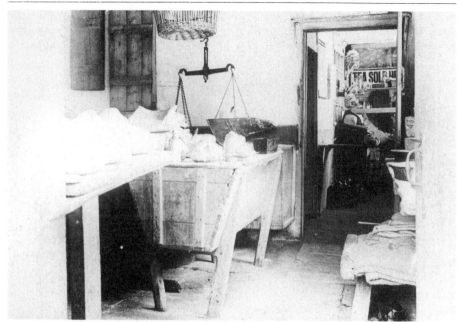

A BAKER'S INTERIOR AT WINCHELSEA in the 1890s. Although not identified, this photograph was found in a Winchelsea collection, and a bakery is indicated by the loaves, scales, sacks and the kneading trough with canted legs. Dry grocery goods such as tea were often sold by bakers. Andrew Johnson was succeeded as baker in Mill Road by James Homard during the 1890s.

A BAKER'S DELIVERY AT BREDE. Sid Cruttenden driving a dog-cart for the Brede Baker, Ernest Oliver, c.1910.

ELLIS BROS, IRONMONGERS, RYE, c.1906. The business occupied substantial premises at the eastern end of the High Street, with an impressive entrance and double shop-frontage. This site had been an ironmonger's since the mid-eighteenth century, when David Guy gave his name to Guy's Cliff to the east, subsequently named Hilder's Cliff after the nineteenth-century ironmongers. The shop was taken over by Ellis Bros of New Romney, builders and builder's merchants in the 1900s, and ran in conjunction with a builder's business they also established in Rye.

DEACON'S LIBRARY AT NO. 26 HIGH STREET, RYE, in the 1900s. Another long-established business serving a wide area, the library began in the eighteenth century as a printer's, stationer's and bookseller's. The circulating library, a common combination with printing, charged 2*d.* per volume per week in 1898, or one guinea per annum with free loan of magazines. The business also dealt in artists' materials, postcards, pottery, sports equipment, musical instruments and sewing-machines. It was a newspaper office and a publisher of a guide to Rye, as was a rival printer, Adams & Son.

THE START OF A SMALL BUSINESS. Mrs Jinny Rhodes at her newsagent's shop, opened in the front room at No. 3 Tower Street in the late 1920s. Mrs Rhodes, wife of Walter 'Jerry' Rhodes, a shrimper, built upon the example of her brothers, who had carried on a newspaper delivery business in Rye from a handcart.

THE BUSINESS EXPANDS. In a time of growing literacy and mass readership of newspapers the business succeeded. After a few years, Mrs Rhodes moved to the adjoining No. 4 Tower Street, presumably to take advantage of the shop-front.

A PUBLIC SPEAKER AT THE GEORGE HOTEL, HIGH STREET, RYE, before 1899. The George was the leading hotel in Rye, used for many functions including civic dinners, auctions and meetings of all kinds. An assembly room was added in 1818 for dances and concerts. Bennett's horse-drawn omnibus travelled daily to Tenterden, via the South Eastern Railway station at Rye.

THE CINQUE PORTS HOTEL AND ASSEMBLY ROOMS, c.1910. A coaching-inn built in the early nineteenth century, the Cinque Ports was the meeting place of several organizations including sports clubs and the Rifle Volunteers. The adjoining assembly rooms were built in the 1860s and, as the 'Bijou Theatre', were a popular venue for entertainments until 1931.

THE MINT, RYE, c.1870. The photograph shows no fewer than three inns, with only one intervening building. The Foresters Arms, The Swan, and The Standard all opened in the mid-nineteenth century and were among twenty-one public houses recorded in the town in 1874. The number was reduced under legislation passed in the 1900s.

A COUNTRY INN – THE WILLIAM THE CONQUEROR, IDEN, c.1900. Most villages had two public houses, the landlord sometimes pursuing a second occupation such as saddler or carrier. The public house was a base for Friendly Societies in addition to being a venue for games and social life. The Dover brewers, Leney & Co., bought Bowen's Eagle Brewery at Rye in 1900.

RYE POST OFFICE, c.1905. Rye had the status of a head office, with a money order facility, a savings bank and a telegraph office. The improved postal service and increased correspondence in the Victorian period led to several moves before a new office was built at Nos. 18, 19 and 20 High Street in 1902. The post office moved to its current location in Cinque Ports Street in 1960.

A VILLAGE POST OFFICE in the 1950s. Arthur Wareham behind his counter at Peasmarsh Post Office and Stores.

A VILLAGE POSTMAN in the 1920s. George Eldridge walked from Playden Post Office and delivered to East Guldeford and part of Playden. He is here seen outside Scots Float House, Military Road, Playden. His tunic was worn largely unbuttoned, displaying his waistcoat and watch-chain.

A HORSE-DRAWN MAIL-CART, probably in the 1900s. The cart carried mail from Rye Post Office to Northiam before the advent of motor vans. The dog probably accompanied the driver as a companion and guard dog. In the 1880s letters were taken on from Northiam to Brede every morning.

JAMES COLEMAN VIDLER (1825–1898) took over the auctioneer's business run as a sideline by his father, John Vidler, a merchant at The Strand in Rye. He developed the business to include farm and trade valuations, house agency in Rye and Hastings, and land agency for several rural estates. Elected Mayor of Rye on three occasions, his geniality and humour earned him the title of 'the most popular man in Rye'.

RYE CATTLE MARKET, probably in the 1930s. The market was established on its present site next to the railway in the 1850s. Normally a fortnightly fatstock sale, the animals being sold for slaughter, the photograph shows an autumn store sale of animals for further fattening. The auctioneer was Ernest Holden Stutely of Vidler & Co. A policeman attended to prevent any cruelty to the animals by handlers.

NORTHIAM FAIR, probably in the 1930s. A twice-yearly store sale, the fair was started in 1901 by F.T. Lane Howse, a former schoolmaster who had taken up farming and had responded to demand by farmers for a local market. A market for regular sales was laid out near the railway station at Northiam and the business grew into the estate agent's firm, Howse & Co., with offices at Beckley.

LANE HOWSE (1899–1965), son of its founder, took over Howse & Co. in 1932, acting as agent for the Brickwall Estate at Northiam and including timber valuation as a specialization in the firm's business.

THE RYE OLD BANK AND SOLICITOR'S OFFICE, HIGH STREET, c.1890. A bank was founded at Rye in 1790 by the solicitor and landowner, Jeremiah Curteis, a partner in the firm of Curteis, Waterman & Woollett. The photograph shows the original bank on the right (then occupied by a later law firm), and Curteis, Pomfret & Co.'s bank, with ancient cottages adjoining, to the left.

LLOYDS BANK, RYE, in the 1890s. The Rye Old Bank was taken over by Lloyds in 1893, the cottages being demolished two years later to make way for a rebuilt and enlarged bank. This, in turn, was remodelled in 1920.

SECTION FIVE

Public Life

In the last century Rye possessed its own Quarter and Petty Sessions for the administration of justice, and a mayor and corporation for the government of the town. The latter enjoyed a long tradition, splendid ceremonies and regalia and were not averse to having their photographs taken! Both magistrates and councillors tended to be leading business- and professional men in the town.

In the rural area local landowners served as magistrates, while the Poor Law Guardians and, after 1894, Rural District Councillors, were mainly farmers. Rye's position as a centre of local government was reinforced by the fact that all the various bodies met in the town or its outskirts and the part-time officers were professional men with local practices.

THE RECORDER OF RYE AT THE BOROUGH QUARTER SESSIONS, 22 October 1900. Rye quarter sessions were held at the Town Hall to try felonies under a barrister. The Recorder was R.H. Hurst, then aged 83, sitting with two borough magistrates, the Mayor, Frank Jarrett, and Albert Edward Hinds. The Clerk of the Peace was a Rye solicitor, William Dawes.

RYE POLICE, 1911. Standing, from left to right: PC Berry; PC Muggridge; PC Boniface (based at Playden). Seated: Superintendent Whitlock; Sergeant Sinclair. Rye Borough Police Force was taken over by East Sussex County Constabulary in 1889.

A PARLIAMENTARY ELECTION AT RYE, 20 January 1906. The photograph shows the Liberal Committee Room at the Mint. The successful Conservative candidate was George Loyd Courthope, who represented the division until 1934. Before 1885, when the constituency was enlarged, Rye had shared a borough member with seven adjoining parishes, and, in the days of open voting, elections had been riotous occasions.

RYE TOWN COUNCIL OUTSIDE THE TOWN HALL in 1888. Standing, from left to right: Edwin Hollis Pulford (Sergeant at Mace); John Neve Masters, watchmaker; Isaac Longley, grocer; John Holmes, retired shipbuilder; Herbert Verrall Chapman (Mayor); John Amos Woodhams, surgeon; William Neeves, butcher; Isaac Wright, carrier and landlord of The Crown Inn; and William Boon, retired seedsman. Seated, from left to right: Alderman James Coleman Vidler, auctioneer; Kingsnorth Reeve (Deputy Mayor), auctioneer; and Revd A.J.W. Cross (Chaplain), Vicar of Rye.

Three aldermen and three councillors were missing and a second macebearer was either missing or not appointed at this period. The occasion was probably the election on 9 November 1888 when the new mayor and ex-mayor 'generously presented the town with a new scarlet cloth robe, trimmed with black velvet and musquash fur. It had long been known that Rye was entitled to robe her Mayor in scarlet, and the old blue robe was handed down to the Deputy Mayor'. At this period the Corporation dealt with public health and highways and provided the water supply, a fire brigade, street lighting, and allotments. The Mayor was ex-officio a Magistrate for the Borough and, after 1894, for the Rural District Council area. The councillors were all business- or professional men in the town, the first women being elected in the 1920s.

RYE TOWN COUNCIL, 1954. By this date the Council had acquired housing and planning functions and included members who had retired to the area. With the Mayor, Maurice Beevers, on the Aldermanic Bench, were from left to right: Reginald Prebble; Harry Schofield; Henry Wood (town clerk); Brig. Gen. Edward Wace; and David Candler. Below were the Medical Officer of Health and the Borough Surveyor.

A RYE MAYOR-MAKING CUSTOM. The Mayor, Joseph Adams, throwing hot pennies to the children of Rye after his election in November 1911. The sender of the postcard concluded with a description of the venue: 'I guess you will see the balcony sticks out from the celebrated George Hotel where I shall most likely call in a very few minutes.'

RYE BOROUGH FIRE BRIGADE, 1890. A volunteer brigade was formed in the 1860s and occupied part of the Town Hall until 1937. The trio in the centre were, from left to right: the captain, John William Eden, an insurance agent; the foreman, Spencer Southerden, a painter; and the lieutenant, Cuthbert Hayles, a solicitor. The firemen's houses were all connected to a battery-powered electric alarm in 1894.

WINCHELSEA CORPORATION. Largely ceremonial after the 1880s, the Corporation is here seen in procession during peace celebrations in 1919. From right to left, excluding the first figure: Revd Robert Douglas (Rector); Jack Carey (Sergeant at Mace); Dr John Skinner; George Freeman KC (Mayor); Francis Tighe; John Malloch; and Lewis Streeton, a boy scout.

THE BOARDROOM AT THE UNION WORKHOUSE, c.1870. This building, at the summit of Rye Hill, was the meeting place of the Poor Law Guardians, and after its formation in 1894, of the Rye Rural District Council, whose members also served as Guardians. Successor to the Rye Rural Sanitary Authority and to the Rye Highways Board, the council was known as the 'Farmers Club' because of the preponderance of farmers among its members. Anglican clergy, however, also took part, and two landowners, a grocer and a carrier, were among the members in 1898. There was for many years one lady member of independent means, Miss Curteis, who was followed by her niece, Miss Burra. Apparently of a parsimonious nature, the council, of which no photograph survives, did not always see eye-to-eye with Rye Corporation, notably over joint repairs to Rye Harbour Road in the 1920s. The Sanitary Surveyor to the Council for many years was Edward John Cory, a partner in Reeve and Finn, auctioneers and estate agents, of Rye and Lydd.

NORTHIAM PARISH COUNCIL, 1946. The Chairman, Captain A.R.J. Cyster, and members of the Parish Council laying the first bricks of twenty-four permanent council houses at Coplands Rise. The members included the rector, Revd O.E.J. Foster and the contractor, W.E. Perigoe. In a time of post-war rebuilding, parish councils had been taking part in housing surveys.

A COUNTY COUNCILLOR. East Sussex County Council was formed in 1888, with responsibilities for main roads and the police, and for education after 1902, and the Poor Law and all roads after 1929. Henry Curteis Burra (1870–1958) of Springfield, Rye Foreign, qualified as a barrister but, having inherited his father's estate (see overleaf), served as a magistrate and county councillor for Winchelsea. He was later an alderman and the Chairman of the Council.

A GARDEN PARTY AT SPRINGFIELD, RYE FOREIGN, c.1885. From left to right: Henry Burra; Miss Mary Burra; Miss Ramus; Richard Burra (?); Miss Denise Burra; Bertie Ramus; Miss Frances Burra; Revd Charles Meade Ramus; and Miss Ramus.

The parson and squire were influential in many villages. In addition to his economic power, the squire acted as magistrate in the rural area and often took an interest in social improvements. Henry Burra (1835–1886) was unusual in combining activities as squire of large estates in Sussex, Kent, Lincolnshire and Scotland with those of a banker and public figure in Rye. He won popularity as an impartial chairman, keen cricketer and Captain of the Rifle Volunteers, and served as a magistrate, town councillor and leader of the Conservative Party in Rye. In the words of a Rye historian, 'his purse and time had been at the service of every deserving cause.'

The clergy were often men of distinction in secular fields. Charles Meade Ramus (1821–1895), rector of Playden and East Guldeford, was also an inventor, interested in 'engines of warfare, particularly torpedoes', who worked on designs for a submarine and tested a prototype hydrofoil, 'the Polysphenic ship, which by means of proposed inclined planes was to become the speediest in the world.' The 'ship' was stolen and burned by bonfire-night revellers in Rye.

REVD GEORGE AUGUSTUS LAMB, DD (1781–1864), rector of Iden, Playden and East Guldeford for 57 years from 1807 to 1864, was active in pre-Reform politics in Rye, being the last Patron of the Borough, controlling elections for the government. An opponent described his 'superior intellect, capable of commanding the attachment of his partisans, and of directing their energies to his views. His eloquence was not to be equalled in this locality.'

REVD JOHN LOCKINGTON BATES (1839–1923), successor to Dr Lamb, was also rector of Iden for 57 years. He was an international financier of 'remarkable and outstanding abilities', employing his son as curate while he spent time in the City and in America, where he financed railways. He and his wife were keen archers, founding a club at Iden Park called 'The Archers of the Ancient Towns'.

BELL-RINGERS AT IDEN CHURCH in the 1900s. From left to right: Fred Wells; Ted Coleman; Bill Cloak; Ernie Briant; George Wood; Henry Dive; Bill Wood; and Billy Clark. The formidable figure in the centre was Mr Bartholomew, presumably captain of the ringers.

THE VERGER AT RYE CHURCH, 10 July 1913. Charles Price was listed as verger from 1894 to 1924. Village churches invariably employed a parish clerk or sexton to care for the church, dig graves and assist at services.

A THREE-DECKER PULPIT AT PLAYDEN CHURCH, before 1898. Dating from the eighteenth century, and associated with box pews and a western gallery, such fittings did not often survive Victorian church restoration. The pulpit was arranged on three levels. The clerk read the responses from the lower; the parson conducted the service from the middle and preached from the upper.

RYE BAPTIST CHURCH OPENING CEREMONY, 1910. Long established in Rye, the Baptists moved from an eighteenth-century chapel in Mermaid Street to a new building in Cinque Ports Street. The notice refers to a public meeting and a sermon by the Revd John Wilson.

THE BICENTENARY OF WESLEY'S BIRTH. Celebrations at Winchelsea, Wednesday, 24 June 1903. Winchelsea Wesleyans were gathered under the ash tree under which John Wesley preached his last open-air sermon on 7 October 1790. Methodism was established early in Rye and Winchelsea, and by 1903 there were Methodist chapels in nearly every village.

RYE GRAMMAR SCHOOL BOYS IN 1908. The school was an independent charitable foundation dating from 1638. Aided by the County Council, it moved from the original building in the High Street to new premises in The Grove in 1908, at the same time admitting girls for the first time. The later uniform of brown cap and brown blazer with blue trimmings appears to be represented among other clothing.

RYE BOYS BOARD SCHOOL, c.1880. The school was built as the Mermaid Street National School for 300 boys and girls by the Anglican Church in 1867. It was merged in 1876 with the Red Lion Board School in Lion Street, which had been built following the foundation of a school board to amend deficiencies in the voluntary system. The Lion Street School was attended by girls and infants.

IDEN SCHOOL, c.1917. Built in 1868 as a national school for 106 children, the school closed in 1930, due to falling numbers. The school at Playden was selected to remain open as it took the children from the Rye Union Workhouse in Rye Foreign.

SCHOOL GROUP AT PLAYDEN, probably in the 1900s. The workhouse boys may be recognized by their dark jerseys and, in one case, pugnacious expression.

SECTION SIX

Winchelsea

The first Winchelsea was gradually lost to the sea in the thirteenth century, and a new town was laid out on a hill by Edward I on a grid plan. Many of the medieval public buildings survive, including the partly ruined church and three gates. Numerous vaulted cellars indicate the former extent of the town's wine trade. Winchelsea lost its importance as a port at an early date, due to silting in its harbour, and by the late nineteenth century, the town occupied only 12 of the 39 blocks originally laid out. From this period it shared Rye's popularity with authors, artists and visitors. In the 1880s Winchelsea lost both its borough and, as an enclave within Icklesham, its civil parish status. A Corporation remained to administer charities, as did a detached part of the parish, a relic of the submerged old Winchelsea, which was later incorporated in Camber.

THE STRAND GATE in the 1890s. The horse-drawn road-roller was led by William Field, who was christened in Winchelsea Church on 11 February 1811 – a reminder that not many people could retire from work at this period.

THE COURT HALL AND WESLEY'S TREE. This fine photograph is believed to have been taken in 1852. If so, the top-hatted figure may have witnessed Wesley's sermon under the tree in 1790. By this period the fourteenth-century building, used as the Court Hall from 1587, had passed out of Corporation hands. It was presented to the town in 1890. The tree was uprooted in 1927.

THE NEW INN, 1905, depicting a very quiet street in a small community of around 600, in marked contrast to bustling scenes in Rye. The sign on the side wall reads 'Carriages for Hire'. The New Inn family hotel was occupied by Mrs Elise Mary Kenward in 1899.

GERMAN STREET in the 1890s, following alterations to the Court Hall. The vehicle was a water-carrier. In 1890, the town was 'at present supplied with water from pumps only, but the Local Government Board has recently directed the Rye Rural Sanitary Authority to provide the town with an adequate supply of water and carry out an efficient system of drainage, and these works will shortly be commenced.'

THE PIPEWELL GATE in the 1890s. At one time also known as the Landgate or Ferry Gate, the original gate was destroyed by the French in 1380 and rebuilt in the fifteenth century.

GREYFRIARS CHAPEL in the 1890s. The ruins of the choir of the chapel of a Fransiscan friary were preserved in the grounds of The Friars, a house built soon after 1819 by Richard Stileman. The ruins were open to public inspection on Mondays.

Around the Villages

The following selection of photographs is arranged as a tour of the villages within the former Rye Rural District. It aims to show the physical character of each village, with consideration of its economic base and the influence of land-ownership.

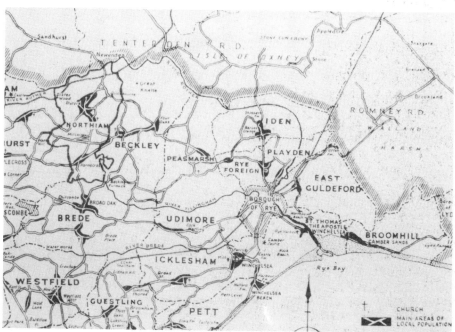

EXTRACT FROM A MAP OF BATTLE RURAL DISTRICT, c.1950, showing the area of the former Rye Rural District Council. Various amendments to the historic parishes had taken place, including the abolition of detached portions. Others were to follow, in particular the merging of Broomhill and the relic of old Winchelsea into the single parish of Camber.

THE POINT, RYE HARBOUR, c.1910. The concrete lighthouse on the Camber side of the river housed red and green tide-signals to indicate depths at night. Masts of fishing vessels may be seen in front of the buildings. The house on the far left had been The Ship Inn, closed down by the local landowner, a temperance writer, around 1900.

RYE HARBOUR CHURCH AND SCHOOL, c.1880. The church was built in the 1850s by landowner Mrs Lucas-Shadwell of The Hall, Fairlight, who also provided a reading room as a counter-attraction to the public houses. As can be seen, much of the village was built on the shingle deposits, exploited for many years by a concrete-works, which supplied blocks for Dover Harbour.

WINCHELSEA BEACH in the 1930s. Winchelsea Beach grew up largely between the wars on the site of Smeaton's unsuccessful new harbour and on shingle ridges. The photograph shows the channel bed, begun in 1761, the Coastguard Cottages, beach huts, visitors' cars and plot-land bungalows on the bank. Two cafés and a dance-hall were listed in 1934.

EAST GULDEFORD CHURCH in the 1890s. The parish was reclaimed from tidal marshland in the fifteenth century by the Guldeford family of Benenden. The small population (137 in 1901, and fewer today) gained their living from sheep farming. The unusual brick church was consecrated in 1505. The children were blackberrying next to a marsh dike or drainage ditch.

CAMBER in the 1920s. Another plot-land village on the coast, uncontrolled development at Camber caused some concern to the authorities. Bungalows may be seen on the dunes with army surplus bell-tents beyond the road. On the right can be seen the Memorial Hall and the church, the latter built by Mrs Lucas-Shadwell in the 1900s.

THE ROYAL WILLIAM, CAMBER, in the 1890s. Built around 1807, the inn served fishermen from the nearby Rye Harbour. The model was carved by the first licensee, William Morris, ship's carpenter on the sloop *The Royal William*. The inn burned down around 1900. This photograph may be dated to after 1894 by the golf caddy in the foreground.

MAIN ROAD, PLAYDEN, AFTER A SNOWSTORM in March 1909. Playden was a small scattered parish on the hill north of Rye. It shared its main road with Rye Foreign. The photograph shows Dick Mills on the left and Henry Dive on the right, respectively gamekeeper and gardener on the Springfield Estate of the Burra family.

SALTCOTE STREET, before 1890. Playden contained a deserted medieval settlement of which this fifteenth-century Wealden 'hall house' was the only survivor. The settlement had boasted a chapel, a beerhouse and a ferry to East Guldeford. The house was destroyed by fire around 1890.

THE SCHOOLHOUSE AND CHURCH, IDEN, in the 1900s. A farming village built around a crossroads, Iden possessed the remains of a moated manor-house, destroyed in the seventeenth century. Later ownership was fragmented until the hop-grower, Jeremiah Smith, built up the Iden and Playden Estate in the nineteenth century.

THE HARE & HOUNDS, RYE FOREIGN, in the 1900s. Rye Foreign was part of the parish of Rye not included in the Borough. A separate parish from 1894, it contained a hamlet on the main road to London. The Mission Hall in the background was built c.1890 by public subscription in Rye. The small shop sold lamp oil and 'Day Martin's Blacking'. Note the chicken, loose on the road.

MAIN STREET, PEASMARSH, in the 1900s. The village grew up along the main London Road some distance from the church. Ownership of the parish was more or less divided between the Peasmarsh Place Estate, south of the road, and the Woodside Estate, north of it, the two totalling 4,500 acres. Owners in the late nineteenth century were local magistrates Charles Liddell and Thomas Pix respectively.

A FLOCK OF SHEEP AT BECKLEY in the 1900s. A heavily wooded parish, with a village also built along the main London Road, Beckley had no resident squire, the Great Knelle Estate of 2,600 acres belonging to the Christie family of Glyndebourne near Lewes. Beckley Golf Club ran a nine-hole course in 1917.

AN EXCURSION TO NORTHIAM, 3 June 1909, by a party of Hastings antiquarians. A large and picturesque village, Northiam contained many medieval houses dating from the time of the Wealden cloth industry. It was the centre of the Brickwall Estate of the Frewen family, established in the area since the seventeenth century. The village possessed several shops, a cattle market, and a railway station on the Kent and East Sussex line. The photograph shows two well-dressed ladies walking easily in the middle of the road.

BREDE VILLAGE GREEN, C.1923. The village street in Brede terminated with the church and The Red Lion facing each other across a small green. The horse-drawn vehicle was descending the steep hill to the Brede Valley. Note the teas advertised on the left. Ownership of Brede was divided between the Frewen Estate and independent farmers.

MAIN ROAD, UDIMORE, in the 1900s. Udimore occupied a high ridge west of Rye on the road to Battle, a good location for the windmill. By 1905 the miller was also operating by steam and a tall chimney is visible beyond the mill. The Post Office and Stores are on the right. The parish was divided among a number of landowners.

MAIN STREET, ICKLESHAM, in the 1890s, now on the trunk road to Hastings, but a quiet rural scene when this photograph was taken. The gable of the village school, built in 1858, is visible behind a pile of road-mending stone. A forge on the right was at one time part of the manufacturing and merchant's business of H.J. Gasson of Rye.

ICKLESHAM, c.1910. The Volunteers in marching order were probably led by Ashton Selmes of Rye. On the right were Cheyney's Almshouses, founded in 1611 and rebuilt in 1842, while the Methodist chapel can be seen in the distance. Icklesham extended for six miles to the mouth of the Rother at Rye Harbour. In 1885 the main landowners were the Brisco and Lucas-Shadwell families of Guestling and Fairlight respectively.

SECTION EIGHT

Farming

In the mid-nineteenth century, Rye was the centre of a flourishing farming area. In his heyday, one of the mayors, Jeremiah Smith, farmed 3,000 acres and was the largest hop-grower in England. In addition to hops, which left a permanent mark on the landscape in the form of conical oast-houses, wheat and sheep were important, the latter especially on the Marsh. Cattle farming and fruit-growing tended to increase with the decline of hops in the late-nineteenth century. Extensive woodlands in the Wealden parishes provided employment in the winter and supplied materials for many uses including building, shipbuilding and tanning.

HAYMAKING AT IDEN in the 1900s. A large work-force gathered for this photograph, with liquid refreshment being provided in a stoneware jar. The contraption on the right was a horse-drawn rake, presumably for turning the hay for the last time before loading into the wagon.

A SHOW BULLOCK AT IDEN in the 1900s, showing Richard Coleman (1856–1935), farm bailiff to Bertram Ramus at Elms and Bosney Farms. A tenant on the Iden and Playden Estate, Ramus was allegedly dispossessed by the agent due to a disagreement between their wives. The holding was regarded as a model farm, all gates and hedges being kept in order and wet weather work provided for the men.

GERTRUDE COLEMAN HAND-REARING A LAMB at Bosney Farm, Iden, c.1910.

SHEEP-SHEARING BY HAND in the 1890s at Elms Farm, Iden. The tar-boy on the left treated sheep accidentally injured during the shearing.

SHEEP-SHEARING BY MACHINE in the 1940s. As a policeman (see page 68), Stephen Muggridge had long cherished a wish to retire into farming. This ambition was realized when he took the tenancy of Rolvenden Farm, Rye, on the Burra family estate.

AN OX-TEAM NEAR HASTINGS in the 1890s. Probably taken at Guestling, the smoke of an engine on the railway line can be seen in the background. Oxen were often used on the heavy, clay soils of the Weald, being steadier than horses.

HORSE-DRAWN PLOUGHING NEAR RANDOLPHS LANE, PLAYDEN, in the 1920s. From left to right: Alfred Mills; Billy Clark; and Frank Wood. Blue Cottage in the background was built in 1794 and used as one of the Poor Houses for Playden before the Union Workhouse was built in 1844.

HAND-REAPING AT BREDE in the 1920s. The men were cutting oats with sickles, probably to make a road into the field for the reaping-machine. Note the use of a stick to control the crop and prevent injury to the legs. The figure in the centre, wearing a necktie and holding a sharpening stone, was probably the farmer or foreman. The younger man on the right was Harry Pepper.

THRESHING AT WINCHELSEA in the 1890s. The crop was stored as sheaves on one side of the barn and threshed on a timber floor in the centre, the doors normally being open to allow the chaff to blow away. Although steam-threshing was increasingly common, threshing by hand was still carried out at Iden in the 1900s. The lettering on the sacks indicates that the farmer was Walter Fuller of Mill House.

BUILDING A HAYSTACK AT BOSNEY FARM, IDEN, probably in the 1920s. The horse-drawn hoist was devised by the farm bailiff, Richard Coleman. The oast-house in the background was disused after 1908.

HAYMAKING AT RYE in the 1900s. Nine people were at work, including a well-dressed woman and a child. The land near Ferry Road was probably hired from the railway company, for seasonal mowing and grazing. The large gable of Gasson's office and stores in Cinque Ports Street can be seen below the church.

APPLE-PICKING NEAR RYE, probably in the 1900s. Fruit-growing was not widespread in the Weald before the late nineteenth century. Note the wide ladders and timber scaffolding, used for hanging baskets and to prevent damage to the trees. Baskets marked with the farmer's name were laid out for booking and removal in the horse-drawn cart.

A HAPPY GROUP OF BLACKCURRANT-PICKERS AT FLACKLEY ASH, PEASMARSH, in the 1900s. The growing of soft fruit was labour intensive, employing as many women as men. The blackcurrants may have replaced hops on this land, the area of hops having declined nationally by more than half during the twenty-five years before 1909. Blackcurrants were also grown briefly during the 1900s at Bosney Farm, Iden, for the manufacture of dye.

EGGSHOLE VALLEY, PEASMARSH, in the 1900s. A hop-garden can be seen on the opposite slope, the hop-poles being stacked out of season. The hop-plants lasted for about twenty years, being cut down to the ground each year. Individual poles were gradually replaced by permanent holes and wirework after the 1880s.

HOP-PICKING, probably at Icklesham in the 1900s. Hop-picking occupied from four to six weeks between August and October and employed large numbers. The children shown are a reminder of the 'hop-picking holiday' from school, allowed later than normal in hop-growing areas. A mother and children could earn enough to buy winter clothes.

HOP-MEASURING AT LEASAM FARM, RYE FOREIGN, c.1905. The hops were picked by hand into bins at the hop-garden, the poles being pulled up and laid flat for the pickers by 'pole-pullers'. The measurer scooped the hops into a bushel-basket, the women often trying to charm him into packing the basket loosely to inflate the number of bushels. The tallyman on the left is seen holding a ten-bushel bag, the 'poke' ready to receive the hops for transporting to the oast-house. He recorded the number of bushels against the bin number in the book hung around his neck, and often provided the pickers with a wooden tally, notched according to the bushels picked. The umbrella in the background was carried for shade and also used as a receptacle for hops picked by children.

UNLOADING HOPS INTO AN OAST-HOUSE in 1911. The pokes were unloaded directly from the wagon into the first floor of the oast-house, used as a cooling area after the hops were dried. The framework on the left was probably a rack to provide ventilation for pokes waiting for space in the oast-house. The lettering on the pokes identifies the farm as Lea Farm, Rye Foreign (postal address Peasmarsh), occupied by Frank Reeve and bought by him at the sale of the Peasmarsh Place Estate in 1919. The 365-acre holding included 52 acres of hops, a large proportion for the period. The oast-house was demolished in 1984.

PRESSING HOPS AT DINGLESDEN FARM, PEASMARSH, in 1903. After the hops had been dried on a slatted floor over a charcoal furnace, a tall pocket was suspended from a hole in the cooling-floor and the hops pressed in tightly. Originally this was done by a man treading inside the pocket, later by a mechanical press.

WEIGHING HOPS AT BANKSIDE, BREDE, in 1903. The filled pockets were weighed in the stowage below the cooling-floor. They were stencilled with details of the county (including the Sussex shield of six martlets), grower and year. In addition to farming, George and David Miller were wind- and water-millers in Brede.

HOP-SAMPLING AT GOTELY FARM, NORTHIAM, in the 1910s, for James W. Lord by Mr Tedham senior. The sampler was a respected figure who travelled between farms, cutting open pockets and taking small samples which were trimmed into a neat block and transported to London for judging before purchase from the grower. The pocket was refilled, sewn up and reweighed.

DRIED HOPS LEAVING FOR THE BOROUGH MARKET, LONDON, in 1912, from Stream Farm, Peasmarsh, on the Woodside Estate, occupied by Henry C. Noakes. His name is just visible on one pocket. Many growers turned the blank side of the pocket outwards to avoid giving information about their crop. The hops completed their journey by train or barge from Rye.

HOMEWARD-BOUND LONDONERS on their way to the railway station. Hop-picking was the annual holiday in Kent and Sussex for thousands of Londoners who made up the shortfall in local labour and were often accommodated in permanent 'hoppers' huts'. At the end of the picking at Bosney Farm, Iden, in the 1900s, the hoppers went one-by-one up the steps of the oast-house to be paid and to have a glass of gin.

THE END OF AN ERA. Albert Paine in 1956, with the last load of hops to be taken to the oast-house at Moat Farm, Iden, from traditional picking. After this date the hop-bines were taken complete to a building for picking by machine.

TRADITIONAL WOODLAND in the 1890s. A coppice with standards, cleared every few years to make the poles and brushwood stacked in the background. The standards, usually oak, were allowed to grow to maturity for building or shipbuilding purposes and produced bark (stacked in the foreground), which was used in tanning, and was one of the main cargoes sent from Rye. Bark was removed from poles to prevent beetle attack.

A CONIFER PLANTATION in the 1920s. From left to right, farmworkers, Fred Catt, Charlie Catt, and their father Will Catt, are seen trimming the side branches from felled trunks. In contrast to the coppice, the land required replanting after felling. Woodlands provided additional employment, especially in winter.

A STEAM SAWING-ENGINE in the 1920s. Members of the Crouch family, Brede woodmen, in Whiteland Wood, Westfield. From left to right: Norman; Will; and Kay. The engine drove a circular saw by means of a long belt, the trunk being moved on planks laid over rollers.

A TIMBER-TUG AT BREDE, 1930. A team of eleven horses towing an oak, four feet in diameter, past Brede Place on a 'tug', or low trolley. Such trees had been much used for shipbuilding in Rye and were transported by this method to the shipyards.

CHARCOAL BURNING AT NORTHIAM, c.1900. Charcoal was used in hop-drying and two oast-cowls can be seen in the background. The burners travelled between farms, covering a 'clamp', or mound of wood, with turf, moss and earth, and using buckets of water to keep it smouldering for several days without burning.

CRICKET-BAT WILLOWS AT NORTHIAM in 1911. The trees had been planted at Crockers Farm, bought by James Moreton Lord in 1900. The sign reads: 'Trees Planted 1901, Young Sets Selected by J.W. Stockdale, Trees felled Nov. & Dec. 1911. J.W. Stockdale, Harold Wood, Essex.' Bats were made locally at Robertsbridge, and the timber was also used to make Sussex trug-baskets. The farm extended into the low-lying Rother Valley.

POLLARDED WILLOWS AT NORTHIAM in the 1890s. The trees were cut about six feet above the ground to produce successive crops out of reach of grazing animals. They were planted beside water – a reminder that every resource on the farm was put to good use. The two boys and the ducks are seen by a shepherd's bridge, leading to an old orchard with new planting in the background.

SECTION NINE

Road and Rail

The importance of water, both sea and navigable river, as a means of transport has already been seen. The link between the port and town and their market areas was the road system, still under the control of turnpike trusts and parishes at the start of the photographic period.

The railway took some goods away from both the port and roads from 1851 but opened the town to new influences and business interests, and later provided a stimulus to tourism. Local journeys were made by horse-drawn vehicle, represented in the photographs by local carriers and farm wagons, as well as by private transport among the better off, and commercial vehicles were used for excursions from an early date.

PLAYDEN TOLL-GATE AT THE PEACE & PLENTY, 1872. A turnpike trust took over the main London road between Rye and Flimwell in 1762 but, in common with others, suffered from railway competition and was wound up in 1872. The cart from the adjoining farm was the last vehicle to pass through the gate. The public house started as a beershop in the 1860s and was largely rebuilt in 1903.

THE WINCHELSEA ROAD TOLL-GATE in the 1890s. Built by the military authorities on a new route to Winchelsea in conjunction with the Royal Military Canal, the road was completed around 1808 and remained in military hands until 1926. The gate stood at the junction with Rye Harbour Road.

A FATAL MOTOR ACCIDENT AT THE MILITARY ROAD TOLL-GATE, PLAYDEN, 27 May 1908. Also part of the Royal Military Canal between Pett and Hythe, the road from Rye to Appledore retained a toll-gate long after their removal from other roads. The gatekeeper's wife, Mrs Thomas, was hit by the car while opening the gate.

A LANE AT WINCHELSEA in the 1890s. Minor roads were maintained by the parishes and the Highway Board until Rye Rural District Council took over the responsibility in 1894. 'Lengthsmen' were employed to maintain a few miles of road each. Overhanging branches were the responsibility of adjoining owners and in 1879 a member of the Highway Board complained that 'at one part of Northiam [he] could hardly drive along beneath the trees without having [his] hat knocked off.'

ROAD-MENDING AT PEASMARSH in the 1920s. The contractors, possibly assisted by council lengthsmen, were Reeve & Selmes of Rye, who also undertook steam-haulage, -threshing and -ploughing. A foreman or inspector had arrived by motor cycle. Note the ex-First World War army uniform.

A FARM WAGON AT RYE, c.1910. Two carters from Oxenbridge Farm, Iden, pictured at Fishmarket Road, probably on their way to Stonham's warehouse at The Strand with a load of grain, avoiding the busier Cinque Ports Street. This area, on the outskirts of Rye, was then recently developed when, in 1859, Cliff Cottage was occupied by Edward Bayley, a master mariner, and the cottages on the right by Jesse Lee and his tenants. The warehouse was built after 1907 on the site of Taverner's wool warehouse and tanyard. The advertisement hoarding relates to H.J. Gasson's 'Fancy tents and marquees, garden and tennis bordering nets', part of a diverse business built on government surplus goods and the manufacture in Rye of tarpaulins and nets.

A WINCHELSEA CARRIER in 1911. Lewis Streeton was one of three carriers who ran a daily service to Rye; one of the others also travelled to Hastings on three days in the week. Streeton was a publican as well as a carrier, a common combination, and is here pictured outside his Salutation Inn in Mill Road with members of his family.

A MOTOR LORRY AT RYE. John Jempson (right) founded a motor-haulage firm in Rye in 1924, having worked in his father's horse-haulage business. The photograps shows hops on a 'J' type Thorneycroft lorry, bought in 1926, in front of the family home, Ebenezer Cottage, at the firm's yard at The Strand.

DRIVING OUT IN STYLE IN THE RYE AREA, c.1860. A party of well-dressed excursionists in a hired wagonette controlled by two post-boys, each riding a horse and wearing the white 'Miller' hat, short jacket and steel boots, left over from the coaching era. The wagonette was an open carriage with one or two crosswise seats in front and two inward facing seats behind.

A WORKS OUTING in the 1910s. Motor charabancs outside the Cinque Ports Hotel during a visit to Rye by employees of the East Kent Brewery. Horse-drawn passenger vehicles were earlier victims to motor competition than their freight counterparts.

THE RYE HARBOUR AND CAMBER BUS in the 1920s. Pictured at the rebuilt Royal William at Camber, the service was run six times a day and at weekends by Wright and Pankhurst, also haulage and removal contractors and taxi operators. The firm's buses were decorated with local scenes painted on the rear. In 1930 the firm sold their bus routes to the East Kent Road Car Company.

A RYE MOTOR TAXI in the 1910s. The taxi was run by Wright and Pankhurst from the yard at their 'Fireproof Furniture Repository' in Tower Stret, Rye, built in 1907. The firm was described as motor-car proprietors from 1911 and later operated 'first-class motors for hire'.

A PRIVATE OMNIBUS AT LEASAM HOUSE, RYE FOREIGN, during the occupation of the house from 1885 to 1903 by Col. Arthur M. Brookfield, MP for Rye. This vehicle was often used in country houses to transport visitors and luggage from the railway station. In a period of nostalgia for the coaching past, the driver was Captain Cruickshank, apparently a guest at the house. The house had been built around 1800 by Jeremiah Curteis, solicitor, town clerk and founder of the Rye bank, for the occupation of his daughter, Anne, and her husband, Samuel Russell Collett. Sold to Brookfield in 1885, it was extended and refaced in 1903 by the subsequent owners, Admiral Sir George and Lady Maud Warrender.

A FARMER'S WIFE ON HER WAY TO RYE in the 1900s. Mary Ann Chittenden, wife of George Chittenden of Boonshill Farm, Iden, and her sister, Rachael, pausing for the photographer at Military Road, Playden, in a governess cart, which had a rear door and step suitable for children. These vehicles remained popular until the 1930s.

A RALLI CAR AT RYE STATION APPROACH, c.1910. Popular in rural areas until the Second World War, and probably made by a local wheel-wright, the Ralli car was a compact variation of the dogcart, with space for one or two people and luggage. The photograph shows the arched front of the station and, on the left, the station lodge, later W.T. Smith's auctioneer's offices.

A PRIVATE WAGONETTE AT IDEN, c.1880. The vehicle belonged to the Curteis family of Leasam House. Presumably used for picnics and outings, the passengers may have stopped for refreshment at the William the Conqueror, behind the photographer. The house in the background, Partridge, has changed little since the picture was taken. Note the coachman and groom in livery with epaulettes.

THE DAWN OF THE PRIVATE MOTOR CAR. Real affluence displayed in the 1900s at Brickwall, Northiam, home of Edward Frewen, landowner, and Lieutenant Colonel in the East Kent Imperial Yeomanry (volunteer cavalry). Unfortunately, none of the people can be identified. The façade of the house was completed in 1633 by the White family, predecessors of the Frewens.

CHILDREN WITH BICYCLES, probably in the 1900s. This charming photograph was found in a collection of glass negatives at Beckley. The girl in particular is well dressed, wearing jewelry and gloves, and carrying a tiny handbag or purse. Although not used after 1908, the letters 'RS' on the boy's cap may denote Rye Grammar School. The oast-house at Brickfield cottages, Beckley, has one roundel added to an earlier building.

A CYCLING LESSON AT RYE in the 1900s, a period of change in Ferry Road. The Ferry Boat had recently been rebuilt as The New Inn, and houses had been demolished next to the cottages, themselves pulled down soon after. By 1907 a terrace of houses had been built on the two sites.

RYE RAILWAY STATION AND GOODS-YARD in the 1890s. Opened in 1851, the station was on the South Eastern Railway Company's line from Hastings to Ashford. Taken from the foot-bridge at the Ferry Road crossing, this fascinating photograph shows busy sidings, with trucks (one apparently loaded with hops) being covered with tarpaulins, a crane, and a motley collection of empty farm wagons on the right. A horse and van can be seen waiting in front of the goods-shed, beside which a siding led, via a turntable, to Hicks & Sons, wholesale grocery warehouse in Cinque Ports Street.

In the background, figures are visible, standing on the platform beside a steam train about to pull away on the down line to Hastings. The signalling arrangements at this period included a tall signal-post and signal-box near the station, various shunting lights between the tracks, and a signal-box adjoining the lodge.

The picture can be dated to after 1893 by the signal-box opposite the station and, unless the railway company was slow to change the lettering on the trucks, to before the merger which formed the South Eastern and Chatham Railway in 1899. A gate-house had been built next to the gate on the right by 1907.

A TRAIN PASSING OVER THE TILLINGHAM BRIDGE in the 1920s, following the merger which formed the Southern Railway in 1921. The 0–4–2 engine (no bogey, four driving and two trailing wheels) draws a tender, horse-box and passenger coach over the wooden trestle bridge replaced in the 1950s. The windmill burnt down in 1930 and, although redundant, was rebuilt as a shell to comply with the terms of the lease.

AN EARLY ENGINE ON THE ROTHER SWING BRIDGE. Built to enable boats with fixed masts to travel along the river, the bridge was replaced in 1903 to allow full conversion to a double track. The 2–4–0 engine is very similar to that shown on an engraving of the bridge in 1851. Lacking cab protection for the driver and fireman, such engines went out of use around 1870.

THE RYE AND CAMBER TRAM. Remembered with affection by many, the 3 ft gauge tramway was opened in 1895 to serve fishermen and members of the newly-opened Rye Golf Club. Later extended to Camber Sands, the line was crowded in summer with day trippers. The photograph shows a trial run of the first rolling stock, the 2–4–0 tank locomotive *Camber* and a single carriage, at the Rye terminus. Requisitioned in 1939, the tramway was closed after the war.

NORTHIAM STATION. Designed by Holman Stephens, also engineer to the Rye and Camber Tramway, the Rother Valley Railway was opened in 1900 between Robertsbridge and Tenterden (later extended to Headcorn). The rolling stock behind the platform indicates a date before the renaming of the line as the Kent & East Sussex Railway in 1904. A cattle market, corn mill and hotel were soon built near the station.

SECTION TEN

Domestic Life

The following photographs reveal a contrast between the leisured lifestyle of the wealthy, with staffs of servants and spacious homes, and that of cottagers struggling with well-water and bundles of firewood. Housing included estate cottages and speculative terraces, while in town and country ancient timber-framed houses were adapted for craftsmen and farm labourers. With the development of council housing from the 1920s many old tenanted cottages in Rye and the rural area were sold to newcomers in search of the picturesque.

FEMALE SERVANTS AT LEASAM HOUSE, RYE FOREIGN, 1860. From left to right: C. Greenfield; A. Greenfield; S. Cheal (lady's maid); Mrs Mantle (cook); L. Boots (housemaid); S. Colvin (housemaid); M. Ashdown; and A. Gasson. The servants formed a sizeable establishment at the home of landowner and farmer, Major Edward Barrett Curteis. Not included in the photograph was the butler, Stephen Care, who later married the lady's maid, Sarah Cheal.

A CROQUET PARTY AT CHURCH HOUSE, BECKLEY, in the 1900s, a peaceful scene from the years before the First World War. Three fashionable ladies are seen being served tea and biscuits by a maid after a game of croquet on a country-house lawn. Everything indicates affluence and comfort: the lace table-cloths and inlaid table, an elegant kettle on a hot-stand, lace window-blinds, the ladies' hats, the maid's smart uniform and the immaculate garden. It has not been possible to identify the ladies, the house apparently having been let to a succession of female tenants, including for a short period the Misses Comforts' Collegiate School for Girls. Completed in the 1740s (with a later bay window on the left), the house was the home of heiress Elizabeth Waters who shocked local society in the 1780s by marrying her young groom, Samuel Reeves. In the background is Beckley Church with dormer windows dating from the 1880s restoration.

A TIMBER-FRAMED HOUSE IN RYE, c.1870. Thomas House in West Street survived from the sixteenth century with little external alteration, retaining the elaborate projecting windows on the right. Many houses in Rye were affected by complicated sub-divisions resulting in the flying freeholds still found today. These left the adjoining weather-boarded cottage bereft of even a yard. The notice related to Charles Thomas, a popular postman and Deputy Registrar of Births and Deaths, who often read and wrote letters for the illiterate.

A WEATHER-BOARDED COTTAGE AT PEASMARSH, c.1910. Typical of many eighteenth-century cottages in the country, this one had a central doorway with a kitchen on the left (with larger chimney) and parlour or scullery on the right, often with a lean-to at the rear. It stood in a group of 'wayside' cottages, built on the wide road-verges at Flackley Ash Hill, including, on the right, a large encroachment within the road itself.

NEIGHBOURS IN THE TOWN. Two old ladies exchanging gossip on their doorsteps on the west side of Church Square, Rye, in the 1950s.

NEIGHBOURS IN THE COUNTRY. Two old men talking over the garden gate in the 1890s. Note the short smock, trousers tied at the knee, and besom broom, which was placed over a stake and used as a boot brush. The cottages have only recently been identified as the Old Workhouse, Guestling, just outside the former Rye Rural District.

A COTTAGE YARD in the 1890s, an interesting study of domestic arrangements. The well required turning by hand, and the firewood had to be bundled into faggots or chopped on the block in the background.

A COTTAGE GARDEN in the 1890s. A mother is seen hoeing a small garden put to use as a vegetable plot, while watched by a child in the doorway and by the baker's delivery boy. The photograph also shows the back of cottages at North Street, Winchelsea, with the Five Houses, School Hill, in the background.

BREDE PLACE in the 1890s. Built around 1400 by the Oxenbridge family and later extended by them, the estate was bought in the seventeenth and eighteenth centuries by the Frewens of Brickwall, Northiam. The house was occupied by yeoman farmers, bailiffs and farm labourers. Partly restored in 1872, it was not permanently occupied until 1913/14, when Moreton Frewen employed the architect Lutyens to complete the work. The house was gutted by fire in 1979.

COURT LODGE, UDIMORE, c.1910. Another gentry house, Court Lodge had been a secondary home of the Etchingham family since the Conquest. The house was rebuilt after 1479 and, owned by non-residents, the surviving north range was used from 1690 as farm labourers' cottages. These were dismantled and moved to a new site at Groombridge in 1912.

AN OCCUPANT OF COURT LODGE, UDIMORE, in the 1890s. At this period Court Lodge was occupied by James Cooper, farm bailiff to Robert Kenward of the Hammonds, Udimore, and by four farm labourers and their families. This splendid portrait by George Woods shows an old man carrying a billy can and stick and dressed in a long smock, wide felt-hat and gaiters – probably the all-weather clothing of a shepherd rather than a bailiff.

WINTONS COTTAGES, PEASMARSH, c.1913. These estate cottages on the Peasmarsh Place Estate of Charles Lyon Liddell were built around 1906, together with a nearby house in similar style for the estate bailiff, both using sandstone quarried on the estate. Each cottage contained three bedrooms, a parlour, a kitchen, a pantry and a scullery.

SOUTH UNDERCLIFF, RYE, c.1910. Rye was increasingly developed by speculative house-builders from the early nineteenth century. South Undercliff was built in phases: Gordon Villas on the right in the 1880s, Castle Terrace beyond in 1904/5, and Battery Gardens after 1907. The houses were decried as an eyesore, although 'much needed'. Note F.J. Thompson's baker's handcart and the chimney of the Rother Ironworks.

SECTION ELEVEN

Leisure

Rye's active social life is revealed both in the photographs and in local directories. The town possessed at least 36 leisure organizations in 1898, covering sporting, educational, dramatic, musical and religious interests. The villages were equally adept at home-grown entertainment, even the smallest having a cricket or football club and many boasting a village band.

Although some activities, notably golf, were based on social position, many provided an opportunity for both rich and poor, including field sports, annual events, and organizations such as the Boy Scouts and the Womens' Institute. The countryside provided activities for all, including visitors, and was often reached by the railway.

A COUNTRY EXPEDITION. Gathering may-blossom at Winchelsea in the peaceful countryside of the 1890s, probably on the Royal Military Road to Rye. The older lady carried protection against the sun.

A GROUP OF GAMEKEEPERS AND BEATERS ON THE FAIRLIGHT HALL ESTATE in the late nineteenth century. An impressive turn-out of no less than five keepers, twenty-nine men, and nine boys, all provided with livery. At its peak the estate included almost all the land in Fairlight and Pett, with part of Icklesham as far as Rye Harbour. It was founded by William Lucas Shadwell, a Hastings solicitor who is said to have made a fortune from building Martello towers for the government in the Napoleonic Wars. His son built a castellated mansion at Fairlight, from which his wife exercised her care over the estate, building churches and reading rooms, and closing public houses (her young brother had died in a runaway carriage neglected by a groom drinking at an inn). The estate, already reduced in size, was split up and sold in 1917, partly for the residential development now at Pett Level and Fairlight Cove.

FOXHOUNDS SETTING OUT TO DRAW COVER, from a meet at the Broad Oak Inn, Brede, from a postcard sent in 1903. Note the broken farm implements in the foreground, possibly awaiting repair at the nearby wheel-wright's shop.

HARE-COURSING AT CAMBER in the 1900s. A popular sport, here represented by the Rye and East Guldeford Coursing Club at its regular venue, the Royal William Hotel. Coursing involved releasing a captive hare for chasing over a short distance by greyhounds, in contrast to beagling, where the hunt was a much longer process. Many hares escaped from the hounds.

A RYE FOOTBALL TEAM, C. 1910. Apart from Frank Barling, standing fifth from the left, the team has not been identified. The players appear to be wearing the red-and-black shirts of the Rye Town Club, the initials possibly referring to the Second XI. Other clubs of the period were Rye Albion, Rother Invicta and St Mary's.

A CRICKET TEAM AT THE SALTS, RYE. Dressed in the clothes of a previous age, the team may have been an earlier version of the 'Old English Cricketers', Mr T. Sharpe's XI, who were photographed at the coronation celebrations in 1911. The elegant figure on the left appears to be T. Sharpe, next to H.J. Gasson, but most of the players are different from those known to have been present in 1911.

WINCHELSEA QUOITS TEAM, C.1900. Pictured at the present cricket field, the team included a roadman, 'Chummy' Barden (left), a plumber, Ernest Freeman, and a shepherd, Bill Eldridge (the latter two flanking the smocked figure). Quoits was also played among fishermen in Rye, where a four-gallon jar of beer was 'deemed essential for keeping the players eye in'.

GOLFERS AND CADDIES AT RYE GOLF CLUB in the 1900s. A game for the élite, the Rye club numbered a future king (George VI) and prime minister (A.J. Balfour) among its visiting players. Social distinction is evident from the debonair poses of the players contrasting with the rather uncertain demeanour of the caddies.

'RYE ATHLETIC MARATHON RACE, $11\frac{1}{2}$ miles, time 1 h. 10 mts., Oct. 11th 1910'. A regular annual event from the 1900s, photographed either here at the railway station or at the Town Hall. A. Wood, here in second place, was a frequent winner.

RYE REGATTA c.1900. Associated with an annual Sports Day on the Salts, the Regatta was revived in 1888. The boats included sailing-yachts and a steam-launch, with the Monk-bretton Bridge and the Camber tram in the background. Events included races of various kinds, water polo, decorated boats and the slippery pole contest on the bowsprit of a fishing boat.

'TREAT TO THE CHILDREN OF RYE BY H.J. GASSON, ESQ., MAYOR', 1905. Such treats were a regular feature of the mayoral year in the 1900s and included events on the Salts. Taken at the station approach, the photograph shows garlanded donkeys and children in fancy dress, with a goods train, railway water-tower and the cattle market in the background.

PLEASURE BOATS ON THE ROTHER, c.1910. Later operated with a tea-room, the boats offered return trips from Scots Float Sluice, Playden (in the background), to Bodiam Castle. They were popular among visitors and among shop assistants on early-closing afternoons.

BOYS SCOUTS AT RYE, 1911. Founded in 1909, the first Boy Scouts troop in Rye was led by Captain Edward John Cory, a Boer War comrade of Baden-Powell and partner in the auctioneering firm, Reeve & Finn. The troop was reviewed by the King at a national rally, and, Captain Cory having died in March 1911, the colours were presented by his uncle and business partner, Kingsnorth Reeve.

IDEN WOMEN'S INSTITUTE, C.1925. The Iden WI was founded in 1918 as were many others in the district. Outdoor meetings were held in the summer, in this case at Miss Foster's, now Hedgerows, Grove Lane. Miss Foster is seated in the middle row, fourth from the right, next to the President, Dorothy Carter (fifth). Also included are Gertrude Coleman (front left) and Mrs Chittenden (standing second from right), already seen on pages 96 and 121 respectively.

JIM COLEMAN, of Military Road, Playden, with his cello, at Bosney Farm, Iden, in the 1900s. The Coleman brothers (including the farm bailiff, Richard Coleman) would meet at the farm on Sunday afternoons for music sessions. A string band played at Iden at this period under the leadership of the grocer and butcher, Pierce Pettitt, who also advertised stringed instruments under the striking headline 'Violins! Violins! Violins!'

PEASMARSH BRASS BAND in the 1900s. Founded in 1902, the band was taken to many engagements outside Peasmarsh by the village carrier, Ernest Offen, and practised in an oast-house, moving to a stable at The Cock Inn when the oast-house was required for drying hops.

RYE ELECTRIC PALACE, c.1920. Regular mass entertainment began in Rye with its first cinema, opened at the Landgate in 1912, starting with a hand-cranked projector and soon showing recruitment films for the First World War. The building had its own generator (before the introduction of mains electricity to Rye in 1925) to power its lights, including the bulbs forming the lettering over the door. The Electric Palace closed in 1932 when the owners built the first Regent cinema in Rye.

SECTION TWELVE

Bad Times

Poverty and infectious diseases were present or were at least a permanent risk during the period when these photographs were taken, and occupied the attentions of the Guardians and sanitary authorities. Early deaths also resulted from road accidents, which occurred even in a pre-motor age.

Moreover, Rye's geographical location has endangered lives of the town's inhabitants in two ways. Firstly, in times of war, invasion was a constant threat. Volunteers were formed following the 1859 French scare, and in both world wars the district suffered civilian losses from air raids in addition to casualties among servicemen. Secondly, the sea has taken its toll of both lives and property through shipwreck, freak weather and coastal change, notably in the 1928 lifeboat disaster when all seventeen crew members were lost.

A RYE FUNERAL in 1899. A member of 'E' company, the 1st Cinque Ports Rifle Volunteers, David Harry Bourne, was killed at Winchelsea Hill on 26 June 1899, aged 26. His comrades formed an escort party to the cemetery, and the procession attracted many onlookers, including some from the curtained windows above. The shops, all shuttered, included: Knight & Son, tailors; Palmer, grocer; G. Burnham, a plumber; and J. Pearson, a greengrocer.

RYE UNION WORKHOUSE FROM THE AIR, c.1930. Built in 1844 on Rye Hill, outside the town, the workhouse served the parishes of the Rye Union, later the Rural District, under a local board of guardians financed from the rates. The Rye historian, Holloway, writing only three years later, commended its provision for the aged and infirm, and for children, 'whose morals and education are well provided for', but decried its deterrent aspects: 'To the able bodied, but unfortunate labourer it deals out a harsh and unmerited degree of severity and punishment.' The harsh regime included separation of men and women, restrictions on leaving the premises, limited visiting and hard manual work. One old man, shaved for the first time on the orders of the matron, is said to have cried for days.

After 1929, the building was renamed 'The Retreat' and run as a Public Assistance Institution by the County Council. The photograph shows the main wards, with dining-hall and kitchen to the rear, and separate infirmary and laundry on the left. Not included here are the boardroom and casual wards. The latter were for tramps, who were required to hand over their money on admission. It was well known to staff that the money was hidden by the road and retrieved later. On a separate site is the Rye, Winchelsea and District Memorial Hospital, built by private donation in 1922, while to the right is Playden Church, with the parish beyond.

ELDERLY INMATES AT THE WORKHOUSE. Note the uniform, grey frock, apron and shawl. Grey suits were worn by the men.

STAFF AT THE POOR LAW INSTITUTION, c.1922. The term 'workhouse' was dropped after the First World War. Standing, from left to right: Mr Butler (caretaker); Nurse Lloyd; Mrs Butler; Mrs Murrell (assistant matron); a nurse; and Mr Murrell (assistant master). Seated, from left to right: Mrs Cregland (matron); Mr Cregland (master); and a nurse. The small boy was Stanley Murrell.

SELF-HELP IN ACTION, Club Day at Northiam in the 1900s. Always held on the first Thursday in May, the members wore white smocks, possibly emblems of purity, and carried staves in procession around the village, taking in the church and a public house before games on the village green. Associated with slate clubs or Friendly Societies, Club Days died out with the introduction of National Insurance.

WINCHELSEA LACE SCHOOL in the 1900s. Founded around 1898 by Mrs Skinner of Periteau House Private Asylum, the school was a revival of an early nineteenth-century industry, carried out by poor children, who were apprenticed by the Overseers of the Poor from neighbouring parishes. The building survives as the 'Little Shop', High Street.

VOLUNTEER ARTILLERY AT THE GUN-GARDEN, RYE, early 1870s. Formed as an offshoot of the Rifle Volunteers in 1861, the 4th Cinque Ports (Hastings and Rye) Volunteer Artillery held annual prize firings at the Rye Battery until 1873. The battery was otherwise in the charge of a master gunner of the Royal Artillery Coast Brigade. The soup kitchen attached to the Ypres Tower was built in 1870. The corps was disbanded in 1876 for insurbordination, having refused to march home from a match at Hastings, taking the train instead.

RIFLE VOLUNTEERS AT LEASAM CAMP, RYE FOREIGN, 1889. The Rye 'E' company of the 1st Cinque Ports Battalion Volunteer Rifle Corps was founded in 1885. In 1889 the annual camp of the battalion was held at the home of the officer commanding, Rye MP, Lt. Col. Arthur Montague Brookfield. Pictured is the Stretcher Bearer Company. The officers (in plumed hats) were, from left to right: Surg. Capt. Marshall; Surg. Major Juluis Skinner; and Surg. Lt. E.W. Skinner.

FIRST WORLD WAR RECRUITS FROM RYE, UDIMORE AND IDEN, gathered at the station approach, Rye, with their recruiting sergeant. A large number of local recruits joined the Royal Sussex Regiment. One wonders how many of these faces did not return. The advertisements are of interest, two offering accommodation for golfers.

'RECRUITS WILLING BUT WONT' AT WINCHELSEA, c.1915. Standing, from left to right: (not known); Barden, an ostler (with newspaper); (?) Field; Mrs Homard, landlady of the Old Castle Inn; George Gaywood (with cabbage); and Ernest Freeman, a plumber (with mop). Seated, left to right: Dickie Homard, a baker; Jack Gallop, a builder; and 'Smiler', a painter. It seems likely that the men were willing to serve but were rejected on the grounds of their obvious age.

FIRST WORLD WAR GENERAL RESERVE OUTSIDE RYE RAILWAY STATION. Equivalent to the Second World War's Home Guard, the group is here seen apparently on its way to a rally. One participant wrote to his uncle: 'I was so sorry you were not with us in the Photo ... we mustered altogether between 7 and 800 ... we were the only Corps not in uniform.'

'RYE MEMORIAL CROSS – RYE SCHOOLBOYS HONOUR THE DEAD'. On Monday 20 October 1919, the day after the official unveiling, W. Sprigg Walker, headmaster of the Rye Boys' Council School, led his pupils to the War Memorial, where he urged them to 'treat the Memorial as a sacred emblem, not to play about it or deface it, but to salute it whenever you pass it.'

SECOND WORLD WAR HOME GUARD. The Rye Company of the Home Guard, seen here marching down the Landgate, was divided into five platoons, No. 1 (60 strong in 1940) being responsible for the town. Note the girl on the pavement, oblivious to the by then familiar spectacle of marching men.

BOMB DAMAGE AT THE STRAND, RYE. Most of the buildings on one side of the street were destroyed in a hit-and-run raid by four German fighter-bombers on 22 September 1942. The cinema received a direct hit, killing the assistant manager, and the Methodist chapel was badly damaged. Elsewhere in the town gap sites still testify to the effect of bombing.

COASTAL CHANGE. Martello Tower No 31, late nineteenth century. This site is now below the high-water mark off Dogs Hill Road, Winchelsea Beach. It was gradually undermined by the sea, along with seven other towers between Winchelsea Beach and Cliff End, Pett. Built in the Napoleonic Wars, three of the towers were blown up in gun-cotton experiments in the 1870s, when others were still inhabited.

FREAK WEATHER. Built in 1742 on the sea-shore and later extended, the Old Ship Inn, Winchelsea Beach, was popular with artists and authors and with the aviator Geoffrey de Haviland, who once telephoned an order from near London and landed on the beach thirty minutes later. The inn was wrecked by a high tide and storm in November 1931, though it remained open until a replacement was built in the village.

RYE HARBOUR LIFEBOAT CREW, 1884. The dangerous shallow waters off Rye Bay have witnessed many shipwrecks. The lifeboat came to Rye in 1852, with stations at Rye Harbour and Camber. The latter, one and a half miles from the village, was reached on foot, and the boat had to be manhandled down the beach on skids. Pictured are thirteen crew members, wearing cork life-jackets, with thirty-five launchers and other helpers, including a coastguard.

The *Mary Stanford* disaster occurred on 15 November 1928 when, in appalling weather, the lifeboat was summoned to rescue the crew of a Latvian steamer, the *Alice*. Propelled by oars and a sail, the lifeboat was launched with great difficulty only minutes before news reached the shore that the crew had been rescued. Despite all efforts to recall them, the lifeboatmen carried on searching for several hours before retuning, only to capsize just one and a half miles from the harbour. All seventeen were drowned. After the disaster the station was closed and the area was served by the Hastings boat. The boat-house remains as a testimony to the self-sacrifice of the lifeboatmen. An inshore boat with ship-to-shore radio was installed at Rye Harbour in 1966.

THE *MARY STANFORD* AT NEW ROAD, RYE. After the tragedy, the lifeboat was taken by Rye contractors, Wright and Pankhurst, to the Royal National Lifeboat Institution headquarters at Poplar, London, where she was broken up in 1930. Built in 1916, the boat had been chosen for her launching capabilities on the flat coast in preference to a self-righting craft.

LIFEBOAT WIDOWS AT THE FUNERAL, 20 November 1928. Five of the crew were married, and eleven children lost their fathers. The funeral at Rye Harbour was attended by huge crowds. More than £30,000 was raised by subscription for the dependents; a statue of a lifeboatman was placed over the grave and a stained-glass window commemorates the men in Winchelsea Church.

WRECK OF THE *VAN DIEMEN*, 1895. The vessel, a deep-sea sailing-ship, had run aground at high water and overturned. Many such wrecks were attended by the coastguard, who helped to rescue the crews and salvage the cargoes. In the case of the *Seggeta* in 1887, the cargo included gin, and the coastguard had difficulty in preventing its removal by rescuers.

THE SALVAGE OF SS *CRAGOSWALD*, *c.*1902. Driven ashore in a gale near Jury's Gap Coastguard Station, Camber, the vessel was freed by Rother Ironworks, using a framework of beams dug in under the hull.

SECTION THIRTEEN

Celebrations

The heyday of photography in Rye coincided with a period which included many occasions for public rejoicing, such as jubilees, coronations and peace celebrations. Sports and processions were organized on a grand scale (how the huge committee pictured overleaf functioned is hard to imagine!) and provided an opportunity for many groups to dress up and participate in events.

CORONATION CELEBRATIONS, 1902. '60 of the older girls of the various Sunday Schools will give Tambourine Drills and Marches in costume. Instructor Mr J. Harvey.' John Harvey (holding the flags) was a stalwart of the Methodist chapel. He was also prominent in the 1911 coronation celebrations, when he trained three groups, each of twenty-eight girls, to represent England, Scotland and Ireland in national costumes, with singing and dancing accompanied by the town band.

RYE CORONATION COMMITTEE, 1911. Assembled in the garden of No. 11 High Street, the committee numbered no less than eighty-four, including the Mayor, printer Joseph Adams, John Harvey (standing third from left), Town Clerk Walter Dawes, and Alderman John Neve Masters (standing tenth and eleventh from left respectively).

CORONATION PROCESSION, 1911. One of a number taken at The Mint, the photograph shows a party of dismounted yeomanry. Other groups in the procession included civic and legal dignitaries, the fire brigade, and the Boy Scouts. The notice referred to a cricket match, athletic sports, music by Rye Town Military Band and a fireworks display.

PEACE CELEBRATIONS, THE STRAND, 1919. Although not positively identified, the presence of military personnel suggest that this was the peace day procession on 19 July 1919, when the Peasmarsh Brass Band, town councillors, wounded men in carriages, and returned combatants made their way to the Salts, for a free luncheon followed by fancy-dress events, sports and fireworks.

THE HONORARY FREEDOM OF THE BOROUGH was presented to Admiral of the Fleet the Earl Beatty on 14 January 1920. The Earl also unveiled a memorial in the church to his comrade Admiral Sir George Warrender of Leasam House. He is seen here inspecting returned servicemen outside the Town Hall with the Mayor, Councillor J.L. Deacon.

ACKNOWLEDGEMENTS

I am grateful to Geoffrey Bagley for permission to reproduce so extensively from the Rye Museum collections, to Peter J. Greenhalf ARPS, for photographic work, often at short notice, and to Dr. John Whyman of the University of Kent and my wife, Jean, for reading the draft text and making valuable suggestions. The text was typed by Margaret Houslander.

The following have kindly provided advice and information: John Bell, Clifford Bloomfield, Peter Ewart, Gwen Jones, Frank Palmer, Steve Peak, Brion Purdey, John Smith and Ed Wiseman.

Published sources include old trade directories, local newspapers, and the recent series *Rye Memories*, edited by Jo Kirkham for the Thomas Peacocke School Local History Group.

I am most grateful to the following for the use of photographs (the numbers refer to pages, 'a' and 'b' to upper and lower respectively):

John Bartholomew, Mint Arcade: 21b, 45b, 46a, 57, 60b, 70b, 134b, 140a, 150a, 158b, 159a. Brighton Reference Library: 87a. Eleanor Brodrick: 55b, 74. Ernie Burt: 46b, 142b. Gertrude Coleman: 47b, 49a, 96a, 96b, 97a, 100b, 143. Henry Dive: 61b, 76, 80b, 89a, 98b, 113, 114b. Peter Ewart: 21a, 32, 59a, 59b, 151a. Barry Funnell: 29a. Nellie Goodwin: 20a. Hastings Library: 39b, 49b, 92, 126a; with the following forming part of the John E. Ray Glass Negative Collection which is the property of the East Sussex County Council and many not be reproduced in any form without the prior consent of the Council: 23, 25b, 36b, 83b, 131a. Hastings Museum: cover picture, 6, 17a, 19a, 20b, 24, 33, 37b, 38, 56a, 78b, 84a, 84b, 87b, 94a, 98a, 100a, 109a, 112b, 114a, 115a, 130b, 131b, 132a, 133, 135. Norman Hickman: 153b. Mary Howse: 53, 65a, 65b, 91b, 123a, 126b, 128. Beryl Hutchings: 11a, 11b, 13b, 17b, 31, 44b, 62a, 68b, 77a. Basil Jones: 42a, 48b, 140b, 156b. Iris Maxfield: 121a. Stan Murrell: 146, 147a, 147b. Northiam WI: 85, 107a. Eric Offen: 41, 43b, 47a, 56b, 99, 106b, 109b, 110, 111a, 118a. David Padgham: 14a, 14b, 15a, 78a, 83a, 91a, 93a, 93b, 132b, 137a. Albert Paine: 108b. Frank Palmer: 9, 13a, 16a, 35a, 35b, 43a, 48a, 51, 52b, 55a, 58, 68a, 72, 79b, 97b, 117b, 152b, 158a. Mary Parsons: 122b. Peasmarsh WI: 106a, 129b. Elizabeth Rigby: 63b, 111b, 112a, 148a. Rye Library: 79a, 86b, 102a, 118b, 138a, 138b, 144a, 151b, 152a. Rye Museum: 2, 10a, 10b, 12a, 15a, 16b, 18, 19b, 22a, 22b, 25a, 28a, 28b, 34, 36a, 50, 60a, 61a, 66a, 66b, 67, 69, 70a, 71a, 82, 86a, 88b, 94b, 104, 119a, 119b, 123b, 124, 125a, 125b, 129a, 130a, 137b, 141a, 149b. Rye Museum (Band Collection): 26a, 26b, 27, 29b, 30b, 37a, 39a, 40b, 42b, 52a, 88a, 101, 105, 108a, 121b, 144b, 149a, 154, 155a, 156a. Rye Town Council: 64a, 155b, 159b. Anne Scott: 136. Dick Sellman: 54b, 62b, 102b, 103a, 107b, 115b. Bert Sheppard: 89b. Doug Smith: 54a, 134a. Eric Streeton: 117a. Leslie Stutely: 64b. *Sussex Express*: 73a. Christine Tree: 145. Bert Vidler: 116. Winchelsea Museum: 71a, 81, 103b, 139a, 148b, 150b, 153a. Mrs Wood: 95. The remaining photographs are from the author's collection.